TRADITIONAL CLOTHING
OF THE NATIVE AMERICANS

With Patterns and Ideas for Making Authentic Traditional
Clothing, Making Modern Buckskin Clothing
and a Section on Tanning Buckskins
and Furs

A Raven Primitive Skills Book

by
EVARD H. GIBBY

Eagle's View Publishing
A WestWind Incorporated Company
6756 North Fork Road
Liberty, UT 84310
801/745-0905
Eglcrafts@aol.com

ISBN 0-943604-61-3
Library of Congress Catalog Card Number 00-133430

FIRST EDITION

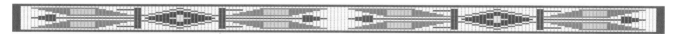

DEDICATION
To My Wife, Paula

B00/45 - 12, 11, 10, 9, 8, 7, 6, 5, 4, 3, 2, 1

TABLE OF CONTENTS

FIGURES AND ILLUSTRATIONS

TABLES

INTRODUCTION

When thinking of Indian Clothing the first thing that often comes to mind is the full buckskins of the Plains Indians with all the feathers, quills, beads and fringe. This image is much of what is popularized in books and movies today. But this is the clothing of only a part of the primitive groups that lived on the North American Continent. Also most of the full buckskin clothing spoken of is dress clothing, with everyday clothing being simpler and usually more crudely made. And for many areas clothing consisted of much less than the full buckskin dress clothing of the Plains Indians.

It was found by the first explorers of the American continent that the native clothing ranged from "no clothes" as Columbus first observed to aprons, grass skirts, breechclouts, buckskin skirts to the full buckskin dress of the Plains Indians.

The main emphasis of this book is to look at the everyday or "work" clothes of the different groups of prehistoric American Natives. However selected items of dress clothing, primarily Plains, will be discussed.

Included are drawings, patterns and ideas for making replicas of traditional clothing; cleaning of buckskin; using buckskin for modern clothing; how some people live in buckskin 365 days a year; and a section devoted to the tanning of buckskin and furs the Indian way. A few other tanning methods will be discussed as well. Included also is a bibliography which will give the reader additional sources to consult.

It is hoped that this book will be a useful reference for those interested in traditional Native American dress and those wanting ideas for using their deerskins and other animal skins.

A person may spend more time and energy in the long run by making their own clothing from buckskin or other materials, than if they had just bought the clothing needed. But by doing so they will have gained something of far more value: He or she will have gained the ability to produce something on their own from available materials, a measure of self reliance and independence from manufactured products, and most importantly a new level of self confidence.

ACKNOWLEDGMENTS AND CREDITS

Aside from the research to find material, many people have played a part in making this book possible.

I would like to thank the following for providing information and/or photographs or allowing me to photograph their items of buckskin clothing:

Jack Stewart the Curator of the Museum of the Badlands in Medora, North Dakota who allowed me free access to the collections in the museum to study, handle and photograph. Jane MacKnight, Registrar of the Idaho Museum of Natural History, Idaho State University, Pocatello Idaho; sagebrush clothing artifacts in the museum. Harold Alshire and Joseph Jastrzembski, buckskin clothing from The Native American Artifact Collection from Minot State University, Minot, North Dakota. Jerry Lee Young of the Idaho Heritage Museum, Hollister; sagebrush and buckskin clothing in his collection. Tony Whitmore; article on Major Beelers Jacket. Linda Martin and Donna Read of Mesa Verde National Park; Anasazi sandals and cordage skirts. Mina A. Jacobs of the Anchorage Museum of History and Art for the photo of an Eskimo woman and child. A special thanks to Jane Bennet-Munro, M.D. Pathologist and Director of the Twin Falls Clinic and Hospital Laboratory, Twin Falls, Idaho for making deerskin into microscope slides and slides into photographs and giving of her time to go over deerskin histology with me. Ken and Brenda Ellis, of Southern Idaho Laboratories for the use of their microscopes. David and Paula Wescott for sponsoring Rabbitstick Rendezvous which has become a living laboratory to meet and learn from others who, among their many other pursuits, are tanning hides and making and living in buckskin clothing. Charles Robbins; felted possibles bags and information about his development of an Ivory® soap tanning method. (Ivory® is a registered trademark of the Procter & Gamble Company and used by permission). Joan Miller; "Baskets for Your Feet" article. Jim Miller; beaver fur mittens. Dorraine Pool; buckskin vest, bra and bikini. Erin and Joshua Sage; buckskin western coat. David W. Crockett; beaver fur hat. Mike Sullivan and his daughter Erin Sullivan; pants, breechclout and dress. Michael J. Powell; capote. Molly Miller; Halter top. Jesus Montes; buckskin and yarn sweater. Dave and Marla Bethke; buckskin clothing. Hawk Clinton and Patti Lopez; buckskin shirt, sandals and boots. Julie Newnam; buckskin skirt and top. Joshua Mendenhall, elkskin and sheepskin vest. Beata Kubiak, wrap skirt. Matt McMahon; Buckskin 365 days a year article. Nancy Coovert a seamstress; tips on skirt patterns and sewing buckskin. Cheryl Vierstra; drawings that appear in the front of some of the chapters. Tamar Raymond, Olivia Plew, Paula Salinas, Genevive Olivas, Mindi Molli, Marty and Dorraine Pool and Neil Gibby for modeling various articles of buckskin and traditional clothing. I would like to thank the Twin Falls Public Library, Twin Falls, Idaho, where the majority of my library research was conducted. I would also like to thank the libraries of the College of Southern Idaho, the Herretts Center Library, both of Twin Falls; the Buhl City Library; the Kimberly City, Idaho Library and the St. George City Library, Utah. A debt of gratitude goes to Monte Smith and Denise Knight of Eagles View Publishing for their suggestions, encouragement, patience and faith in me to put this book together. And finally I want to thank my wife and family for their encouragement and support and for putting up with me during this entire process!

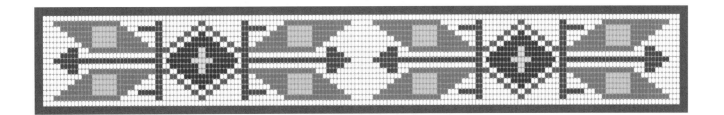

SECTION I

ATLAS OF TRADITIONAL CLOTHING AND MAKING TRADITIONAL AND MODERN CLOTHING AND OTHER ITEMS

THE DRESS

The hides were secure in the frames now... It had been a good hunt. Two deer had been killed, and these hides would make a durable dress. She remembered wanting one last season but no deer had been killed, just smaller animals. The grass and sagebrush bark skirts she has been making wear out fast and they did not give her much protection against the snow and cold in the winter. The season was beginning to change and in two moons the snow would again be falling to the earth. The dress she was making from these hides would be much warmer than her bark skirt, and it would be especially nice with her rabbit skin robe she had made last year.

She thought of her preparations so far: First she had skinned the two deer, thrown the hides into the stream and weighted them down with rocks. Only after the meat had been cut up and hung on sticks to dry, did she have time to pull the hides from the water and begin their preparations. She had next leaned a smooth log up against the crotch of a tree and hung the hides one at a time over it to flesh them. This was done by standing with the log and hide between her legs and scraping the flesh off the hide with a bone from the foreleg of a deer. It had a natural curve and a sharp edge that worked well for removing flesh. After she had fleshed the hides she cut small holes around the edge of each one. Then using string made from plant fibers she had laced and tied each hide into a pole

frame and stretched them out flat. ...they would dry and she would begin scraping the hair off the next day.

When she awoke she got her two scraping tools and checked to see that the stone blades were sharp and tightened the lashings to secure them to the handles. She had left the hides in the sun and checked them several times. By midday they were dry and very tight in the frame and were ready to be scraped. She started on one of them by carefully scraping at the hair near the neck of the animal until she got a small patch of hair removed and the white skin underneath was visible. Each stroke enlarged this white spot, and she thought to herself "this skin is good, it will be a nice dress". She continued the scraping, making sure that the top smooth layer of skin came off with the hair. It came off in small broken curls with the hair attached. This scraping process was continued and by the end of the second day both hides had all the hair removed.

The next day both hides were removed from the frame and again she weighted them down in the stream with some rocks. While they were soaking she went to the back of her wickiup and got the deer brains. They had been scalded and sealed inside a piece of deer intestine and had been stored in the shade of the wickiup since the day the deer had been killed. The wonder of how the brains make the stiff hide so soft came to her mind. And she thought of how

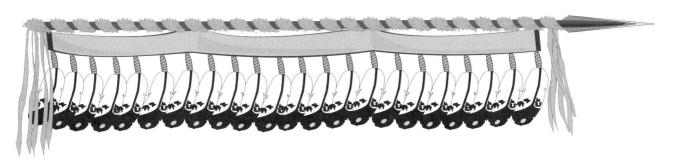

3

nice it would be to have the soft buckskin next to her skin instead of the rough scratchy shredded bark of her skirt. She then put the brains into a large clay pot and added a little water. Then while mashing them between her fingers she heated them over the fire until they were almost too hot to touch. She removed the pot from the fire and submerged the deerskins in the solution and began sloshing them around and working the brains into the hides.

She next wrapped them each one at a time around a small stout tree and twisted them up tight with a stick to wring them out. Then they were re-submerged in the brain solution, and worked as before. This wringing and submerging was continued for several more times until the skins were completely saturated with the brain solution. After a final wringing the skins were hung over a branch of a tree and left overnight.

In the morning she checked the skins early to see how they were drying. They were damp but were starting to stiffen up a little. She stretched and pulled each one for a few minutes. She then fastened a heavy corded rope around the trunk of a tree at the bottom and tied the other end to a branch above her head. This provided a stiff rope that she could pull the hides around to soften them while they dried. To do this she put a hide behind the rope and grabbed it on each side with her hands. She then pulled back briskly on the hide against the rope, and then turned it to a different angle and pulled again. She continued pulling the hide at all angles, sometimes see-sawing the hide across the rope, until they were completely dry and soft. It was late in the afternoon when she was satisfied that both hides were soft and completely dry. They were bright

"It was tempting for her to make the dress from the hides at this stage, but she knew that clothing made from white hides dried stiff after getting wet and required reworking . . ."

white and very soft. It was tempting for her to make the dress from the hides at this stage, but she knew that clothing made from white hides dried stiff after getting wet, and required re-working before being worn again. This was to be her everyday work dress and she did not want to re-soften it every time it got wet, she knew that smoking the hide allowed it to easily re-soften after getting wet. Besides she liked the aroma of wood smoke on her clothes and the tan color was easier to keep clean looking than white skins. She also knew that insects did not eat smoked skins.

Her next step was to punch small holes with a bone awl around the edges of the hides from the rear leg, up the side and around to the other rear leg. She then got some fiber string and laced and tied the two hides together forming a large bag with the rumps being the opening. Then she found a stick to thread between the skins at the neck level and tied a loop of cordage over both ends of the stick so the hides could be hung from a branch over the smoking pit. They were now ready to be smoked.

She scooped a hole for a fire out of the earth about a foot in diameter and about two feet deep. Then she poked a stick at an angle through the ground to the bottom of the hole to allow air to get to the fire. She then brought a basket full of rotted wood and some kindling sticks to the fire pit and started a fire. When the fire burned down to coals she hung the hides directly over the pit from a tree branch, and threw a few handfuls of the dampened rotted wood on the coals. A thick blue smoke began to come off the coals. Then she put the open end of the hides over the fire hole and held the bottom of it down by poking sticks through small holes in the hides into the dirt. She scooped dead leaves up around the bottom of the hides to block the smoke from coming out through the cracks under the hides. The smoke filled the hide bag and began to come out all around from the seams. The coals were watched carefully and she added more punk as needed to keep a heavy smoke coming. More coals were also added from the nearby fire when needed. A pot of water was kept handy to quickly throw on the fire if it got too hot. She did not leave the hide while it was smoking but watched it closely knowing that after this much work she did not want to let it get burned and ruined!

She looked inside one of the seams periodically and could see the hide change from white to yellow and then to brown. She continued the smoking process until she could see the color bleeding through the hide to the outside. Then she turned the hide bag inside out and smoked the other side. When finished the hides were a nice buckskin brown color. She took the lacings out, separated the hides and put them inside her wickiup. Tomorrow she would start on the dress.

After she arose she got the two skins and laid them out flat on the grass. Then with a sharp stone blade she cut across each one from one hind leg to the other in a straight line just a few inches above the tails. From the pieces cut from the rear of the hides she cut a few thin strips of buckskin to use as ties. Then with the awl she punched some holes along the previously cut edges and down both sides of the skins. With the thongs she tied and laced the two skins together, first along the edges where she cut the skin across the rump, leaving a hole for her head, this became the sleeves and neck of the dress, then down each side of the skins to hold the front and back pieces together. These ties could be loosened or removed in hot weather so that the dress would be cooler from the air circulation. The last tie ended several inches above the knee so that leg movement would not be restricted. Her final finishing touch was to take the stone blade and cut fringe on the ends of the sleeves, down each side and across the bottom. This gave the dress form without tailoring or using a pattern.

She removed the bark fringe skirt from around her waist and un-ceremoniously tossed it aside and then pulled the new buckskin dress over her head. She rubbed her hands across the dress and pressed the buckskin against her body. The soft buckskin felt good next to her skin, this was really living - in luxury!

DID YOU KNOW?

Did you know that many types of clothing used by modern white men and certain practices in dress were actually thought of by primitive Native Americans long before modern man came up with the ideas?

Following are a few examples of these customs and practices:

Sandals - Sandals were in widespread use by many groups of Native Americans before the arrival of white men. They were commonly made from skin, rawhide, bark and other natural fibers. In parts of the primitive southwest, sandals were the single most important item of clothing.

Slit Skirt - Native slit skirts were not designed as a fashion statement but rather as a functional item of clothing. Women could easily open the skirt to bare a thigh and then roll fibers on it when making cordage or string. The most famous of the native slit skirts has come to be called the Algonguian slit skirt, worn by Eastern

Woodland peoples.

Wrap Skirt - Generally a wrap skirt was a hide or piece of material just wrapped around the body. A wrap skirt could also be a slit skirt, the overlapping edges forming a slit and used as described above. This was a common type of clothing for several native cultural areas.

Mini Skirt - Again not a fashion statement. The length of Native dresses and skirts varied from very short to ankle length. The length varied not so much because of modesty or to cover the body but on materials available, climate, weather, convenience and other factors. In the mild climate of the southern plains the basic women's garment was a short skirt made from buckskin. Some California groups deliberately cut their skirts into narrow fringe so that they would not restrict movement in doing their daily work which involved a lot of getting up and down from the ground.

Cowboy chaps - Some Plains leggings had wide flaps on the outside and are thought to have been the origin of cowboy chaps.

Mud as clothing! - Records indicate that some California natives covered their bodies with mud to help keep them warm in cooler months.

Nursing bra - John Hunter, a white man who was kidnapped as a small child by Indians and lived with two different groups until adulthood (ca. 1796-1816), described their manners and customs in a book about his experiences. He said that although it was a limited practice some women wore stays to support their breasts while nursing. One can only speculate what their "stays" were like, but they may have been similar to the corsets or bustiers of the day and could have been buckskin or fibers wrapped or laced around the torso to support the bust.

Halter top dress - The Havasupai of the Southwest made a two piece buckskin dress which had a halter top. The front hide had a strap that went over the head and the front of the dress extended over the bust to the ankles. The back of the dress was tied around the waist and extended down to the ankles leaving the back bare. The dress was worn over a short under apron and a skin belt was worn around the dress at the waist.

Grass skirts - Hawaiians weren't the only natives who wore grass skirts. Great Basin, California and other groups commonly wore skirts made from grass, bark strips, and other fibers.

Goggles for eye protection - Before sunglasses and ski goggles the Eskimos were making goggles from wood and ivory that had narrow slits in them to restrict the amount of light that could enter. This allowed better vision in the bright snow and helped to prevent snow blindness. Plateau peoples made similar glasses from buckskin with small slits or holes in them to serve the same purpose.

Sun visor cap - Great Basin peoples made a headdress of rawhide with a bill on it that was similar to a bill cap or sun visor. It had a buckskin thong to tie the hat on under the chin.

Disposable clothing - After seal or whale hunting the men brought the animals to shore to be butchered, the Northwest Coast women then changed into disposable reed or cattail skirts for the job.

Disposable diapers - The Subarctic peoples used sphagnum moss for disposable diapers Other groups also made disposable diapers from shredded tules or other fibers.

How to keep your skirt from blowing in the wind! - Southern California natives made cordage skirts and attached asphalt balls to the bottom of the cords to keep them from flying in the wind.

Armored vests - Californians and other groups made armored vests that were used during warfare. They were made by tightly weaving split branches together with fibers.

Right and left foot wear - Natives had right and left moccasins at a time when white men still had shoes that were the same for both feet.

Nudity and going topless - Did not originate with modern white man in the 60's. Many native groups' normal dress included attire without tops for women and nudity for both men and women. Pecos Pueblo girls went nude and Zuni young women were required to go unclothed until they were married. Children of many groups often went nude for the first several years of their life. This was a normal part of their lives and was not indecent or obscene.

Hair nets - Hair nets are not an original invention of modern man for industry. Great Basin peoples made milkweed or wild flax hair nets to tuck their hair into while working.

Pierced ears - Piercing ears, nasal septums, etc. was very common to the prehistoric American natives.

Mittens hanging on strings - Hanging mittens on strings through coat sleeves is not just a modern way to keep children from loosing their mittens. A common practice by Subarctic peoples and possibly others was to attach their mittens on strings and hang them through their coat sleeves.

Garters - On the plains and in other areas garters were worn by women to hold up their knee high leggings.

Recycling - Native Americans were master recyclers and efficient users of all parts of animals killed. Hides were used for clothing, hair was used for stuffing, bones and antler were made into tools and arrow points, sinew was twisted into cords for bowstrings and thread for sewing, innards were recycled into bags and containers and all other parts of the deer and buffalo found their way into items useful to the natives. Old lodge covers were cut up and recycled into shirts, breechclouts, dresses, moccasins, bags and other items.

Sun Screen - Several groups rubbed grease, paint, clay and ocher on the skin to soften it and protect it from the sun and wind.

Insect repellent - Some Plains groups used bear grease as an insect repellent. It is reported that after bathing they would anoint their bodies with bear grease to keep insects away. Southeastern natives would spread alligator grease and dirt on their bodies to keep mosquitoes away.

Coats with detachable sleeves - Subarctic peoples made parkas with detachable sleeves.

Wearing underwear as outerwear - A unique idea to keep cooler in the summer; just wear underwear! Arctic peoples did just that. They took their winter hide underwear, turned it inside out and wore it for their summer outerwear!

Cultural areas of North America

1. Southeast
2. Northeast Woodlands
3. Plains
4. Southwest
5. Basin and Plateau
6. California
7. Northwest Coast
8. Subarctic
9. Arctic

Figure 1. Nine cultural areas or groupings of Native Americans in prehistoric North America. In the following chapters there are descriptions of the main types of clothing used by the prehistoric and early historic inhabitants of each cultural area.

TRADITIONAL CLOTHING IN THE CULTURAL AREAS

When Christopher Columbus first set foot on land in the new world, his Friday October 12, 1492 entry in the ships log read in part: "At dawn we saw naked people, and I went ashore in the ships boat...No sooner had we concluded the formalities of taking possession of the island than people began to come to the beach, all as naked as their mothers bore them, and the women also..."

This may very likely be European white man's first record of the dress of the natives of the North American Continent. Later, explorers were to learn that the dress of these New World people ranged from no clothes, as Columbus observed, to the finest full buckskins of the Plains Indians. It was also learned that the clothing of the American prehistorics was colorful and quite diverse from one area to another. It appears, as stated by Carl Waldman, that "Climate and available materials dictated types of clothing that served first and foremost the practical purpose of protection, with modesty and concealment of the body rarely a concern".

THE SOUTHEAST

This cultural area extends east from the Atlantic Ocean to Texas and north from Florida into parts of the states of Virginia, West Virginia, Tennessee and Arkansas. The Southeast is wooded, with pine and oak being the predominant trees and cypress in the tropical swamps. There are many streams, rivers, saltwater marshes and fertile soils in the coastal flood plains for crops. The natives lived mainly in villages along the river valleys. They farmed as well as hunted and gathered. Because of the sandy soils their villages were frequently moved to other locations. The coast has many bays and inlets where the natives were able to catch fish and shellfish.

ISLANDS, MEN AND WOMEN'S CLOTHING:
Often naked
Short cotton tunics
Body paint
Feathers on head
Pendants
Gold pieces in nose
Women sometimes wore very small cotton aprons.

MAINLAND, WOMEN'S CLOTHING:
Short skin skirts or twisted fiber skirts
Short wrap around skirts of skin or fiber
Breechclouts
Small covering made from Spanish moss *
Moccasins
Shawls of skin in winter
Face, breasts and back often painted with black stripes

MAINLAND MEN'S CLOTHING:
Breechclouts
Ankle high moccasins
In winter leggings, poncho like shirts and feather robes
Long hair with buckskin braided in
Elaborate tattoos on body

_____
*Spanish moss is a plant with long slender stems that look like hair. It hangs from trees and gets it's moisture from the air. Commercially dried Spanish moss is used as a stuffing for upholstery.

Figure 2. *Florida couple showing clothing and elaborate body tattoos.*

CHILDREN:
Children's clothing similar to their parents
Boys in some areas went naked till puberty and
girls were given skirts and moccasins as soon
as they could walk.
Natchez girls wore a two piece apron made from
mulberry tassel and later knee length skirts.

HAIR:
Women short hair
Men long and braided with buckskin
Hair parted in middle
In some groups the women wore long loose hair
and rubbed grease into it

DECORATIONS:
Both sexes painted and tattooed the body and
wore earrings and pendants.
They spread alligator grease and dirt on their
bodies to keep mosquitoes away.
Women, strings of shell beads

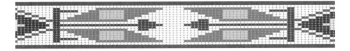

It was on the islands in the West Indies off
the southeast coast of North America that Christopher Columbus first sighted the natives not
wearing clothes. In his travels around the area
he found that a great number of people went
around entirely "naked as they were born," as
many entries in his ships log indicated. But he
also described "...cotton clothes made like short
tunics..." and women wearing a small piece of
cotton in front of their bodies "only large enough
to cover their private parts and no more". In
addition he observed that some painted their
bodies (black, white, and red being the most
common colors), feathers were worn on the
head, pieces of gold were worn in the nose and
various types of pendants were worn around
their necks.

On the mainland of the Southeast the prin-
ciple clothing for men was a breechclout and
moccasins that were ankle high. In areas along
the Gulf Coast the breechclout was extremely
long. In this same area the men wore their hair
long in the back and braided buckskin into it.
Men often had their bodies elaborately tattooed.
In winter they added leggings, poncho like buckskin shirts and feather robes as needed.

In some areas men seldom wore
breechclouts but wore a snake skin around the
waist and tied a fringe of shredded mulberry bark
to it that hung down in the front. Winter robes
were sometimes made from twined mulberry
bark with feathers woven in.

Mainland women wore short skirts (sometimes wrap skirts) made from skin, twisted fibers or woven grass. Some wore breechclouts
or small coverings made from Spanish moss
and loose fitting blouses when needed. Footwear for the women was similar to the men's.
In winter they added shawls of skin and some
wore mulberry bark robes that hung on one
shoulder. Their hair was worn short and parted
in the middle, and their face, breasts and back
were often painted with black stripes. In some
areas colorful feather robes were made from
the green part of mallard heads, with many
pieces all sewn together.

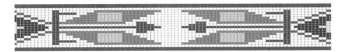

Pocahontas, a Southeastern Indian, married
John Rolfe after the incident with her father and
captain John Smith. In 1616, she and Rolfe
voyaged to England where she was received
as a princess. Her portrait was then painted by
W. Langdon Kiln. This portrait apparently shows
her native dress and was titled "Indian Princess
before she renounced idolatree". The clothing
shown in the portrait is probably dress clothing
and shows a feather robe with a fur edge worn
over the right shoulder and down to the waist
on the left side partially exposing the left breast.
No other clothing is shown. She wears a claw
and bead necklace, some strings of beads and
cordage, a wampum headband, an arm band
and some feather and bead earrings. In an-

other drawing published in 1624 depicting Pocahontas saving Captain Smith, she is shown in what is probably the typical everyday dress of the time period. She is wearing just a front apron of fringed material, possibly fiber or buckskin tied around the waist. No back apron or upper clothing is worn.

Seminole Indians, pushed south in the 18th century by Colonial expansion, originally wore deerskin clothing, but gave it up and began wearing clothing made from cloth obtained from traders. Apparently their unique colorful clothing came about after they obtained small hand cranked sewing machines from white traders. They began to sew hundreds of small strips of cloth together and making their distinct colorful clothing.

The Natchez wove a fabric from the inner bark of the mulberry tree which was used in making clothing.

The Creek wore mostly buckskin clothing but used buffalo hide for moccasins. Men wore breechclouts, moccasins and leggings. Women wore textile or skin knee length skirts with a belt and calf high moccasins and usually wore no clothing above the waist.

Some Woodland and Southeast peoples wore slippers twined from the fibers of a Yucca like plant.

Figure 3. A twined slipper removed from Salts Cave Kentucky in the 1880's. Probably a child's slipper and was made using a plain twine. Photo Courtesy of Joan Miller. (See section on twined slippers).

THE NORTHEAST WOODLANDS

The Northeast Woodlands contains most of the state of Wisconsin, Illinois, part of Tennessee to West Virginia and the rest of the states to the east and north into Canada. This area is heavily wooded with low mountains and rolling hills and bordered by prairies to the west. The East Coast is the eastern border with many beaches and rocky coves. Inland are rivers, streams, lakes and salty grassy marshes. The primary source of material for fuel, tools and shelter was the forests. The animals in the forests were also the main source of food. In addition to hunting and gathering for food the natives fished and farmed. The Iroquois of the area typically lived in communal longhouses while the Algonquian lived in wigwams.

MEN'S CLOTHING:
Buckskin breechclouts
Soft soled moccasins
Leggings
Sometimes skin trousers
Buckskin shirts
Skin robes

Figure 4. *Northeast Woodlands man with breechclout, leggings and moccasins.*

Rabbit skin robes
Feather robes in the South

WOMEN'S CLOTHING
North:
Buckskin "slip and sleeve" or "strap dresses"
Breechclouts
Moccasins
Skin caps
Fur robes

Other areas:
Buckskin wrap around or slit skirts held with belts
Sometimes poncho tops made from buckskin
Soft soled moccasins
Leggings

CHILDREN'S CLOTHING:
Children were usually naked until about ten years old, otherwise they dressed similar to adults.
Some Algonquian children wore wads of moss over their genitals.

HAIR:
Hair was generally worn long by both men and women.
Algonquian women used bear fat to grease hair, their hair was long to the hips and was wrapped with buckskin thongs in one bunch down the back. In other areas women's hair was in one or two long braids.
Both Delaware men and women parted their hair and painted the part red.

DECORATIONS:
Bead jewelry
Embroidered head bands with bangles and feathers added
Necklaces of shells, claws, hooves, bones and etc.
Fox men often had the print of a hand in white clay on the back or shoulder.
Wampum was used to make headbands and belts.
Delaware used snake skin for belts and headbands.

Hopewellians used copper, mica, shell, bone, wood, copper and silver earspools, necklaces of pearls, animal teeth and bone beads.

Ottawa men and women pierced their noses and ears and hung ornaments from them. They also painted and tattooed their faces and bodies.

Algonquian women used fish oil and eagle fat to keep their skin smooth. Red pigment and fat was rubbed on their face, forehead and cheeks and black pigment around the eyes and on the forehead.

Delaware often had elaborate face painting and body tattooing. Animal grease was rubbed on to protect the skin against the cold and sun. They used vegetable and mineral pigments to paint face and body. Several other groups also had elaborate tattoos.

Algonquians used bear grease and oil from walnuts to grease their bodies.

Algonquian men shaved the right side of the head to keep it out of the way of their bowstring and tied the rest of the hair in a knot at the side.

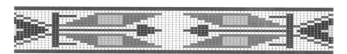

The men in the Northeast Woodlands area usually wore breechclouts, soft soled moccasins, leggings and in some areas along the Atlantic Seaboard skin trousers are reported. They also had skin shirts and robes when the weather demanded. In the South cloaks and headdresses were made from feathers and tattooing was practiced in some areas.
Iroquois men wore one piece moccasins and leggings with no fringe that had the seam up the front. Moccasins in some areas were two piece.

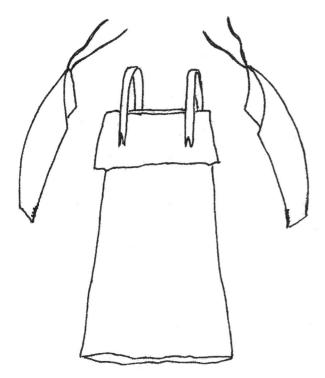

Figure 5. A strap dress sometimes known as a "slip and sleeve dress".

The women in the northern parts wore slip and sleeve tailored dresses, moccasins, skin caps and fur robes. The slip and sleeve dress, or strap dress as some call it, consisted of a buckskin dress held up by two shoulder straps and has been described as being constructed similar to a woman's modern slip. It had separate sleeves that were hooked together at the back and could be worn with the dress when desired.

In other areas women wore soft soled moccasins, wrap around skirts and in warm weather went without upper clothing. When needed poncho or cape like tops were worn, all made from animal skins. The skirt was a rectangular piece of skin that was wrapped around the body, it barely overlapped on the right and has become known as the Algonquian slit skirt. This slit allowed the thigh to be easily bared to roll fibers

on when making cordage. The length of the skirts varied from mid thigh to below the knee. The poncho top has been described as a whole deerskin with a slit cut in the center of the back for a neck hole. It was slipped on over the head similar to a poncho. There were no true sleeves, but the skin extended over each arm similar to sleeves and were not sewn under the arms. The skin could be worn attached to the waist of the skirt or it was sometimes unattached. These skins were cut to be worn conveniently but were not really tailored. Edges and ends were often fringed. They wore short knee length leggings when needed.

In some areas women wore a two skin dress consisting of a skin in front and a skin in back, these were sewn together at the shoulders and held with a belt. Some wore an undershirt of woven nettle fiber under the dress.

Sometimes no clothing was worn by the Algonquian but usually their basic dress was a breechclout or a single or double apron for both men and women.

In northern areas a light jacket or top was worn as protection from the sun.

Shawls and robes served as overcoats and bedding in the wintertime. Robes were made from buckskin, rabbit skin, turkey feathers, or from other skins with the fur attached.

Winter hats were made by wrapping fur skins around the head leaving the top open. This is thought to be the origin of the raccoon skin cap worn by frontiersmen.

Clothing was usually made from buckskin but bear and beaver skin were used and cloth was woven from plant fibers and used for clothing. The Iroquois and Delaware made footgear from corn husks.

In the Upper Great Lakes area clothing was decorated with painted bands of red and brown. Iroquois favored black dyed buckskin.

THE PLAINS INDIANS

The Great Plains cultural area extends from Texas on the south to the Canadian Plains of Manitoba, Saskatchewan and Alberta on the north. It is bordered on the east by the Mississippi River and extends west to the Rockies. This area is the heartland of America and is a vast and almost treeless grassland plain, a perfect grazing land for the American Bison. But there are many river bottoms lined with mostly willows and cottonwood trees. It is thought that at the time of contact the only hunters on the Plains were the Blackfoot in the north and the Comanche in the south. The other people were semi-nomadic farmers that lived in villages principally along the Missouri River. They periodically moved to new sites looking for undepleted soil.

It was with the horses brought in by the whites that the natives developed a new life on the Plains. With these animals the villagers became the well known nomadic hunters of the buffalo. This new lifestyle also attracted other tribes who then migrated into the Plains to become buffalo hunters themselves.

WOMEN'S CLOTHING:

Northern Plains:
Wrap around skirt
Strap dress (slip and sleeve dress)
Side fold dress
T-shaped dresses with belts (two skin dress)
Moccasins as needed
Short leggings as needed, sometimes held up with garters.
Breechclout

Southern plains:
Wrap skirts
Fringed 2 piece skirts
Sometimes poncho like upper garment

Figure 6. *Mans War Shirt, Hidatsa. This shirt belonged to Drags Wolf, The son of Crow Flies High. This Plains shirt is made from brain tanned buckskin and has quilled strips on the front and shoulders. The colors of the quills are red, green and yellow. It has long fringe on the sleeves and along the outer edges of the quilled strips. The triangular neck flap has a quilled design and there is an ermine on each shoulder. Native American Collection, Gordon B. Olson Library, Minot State University, Minot, North Dakota. Photographed by Harold Aleshire.*

• •

Three skin dress
Buffalo robes in cold weather
Boots made from buffalo hides
Tattoos and paint on face forehead and breasts
Hair long and loose

16

MEN'S CLOTHING:
Warm areas- naked
Breechclouts and/or small primitive aprons
Soft soled moccasins
Hip length leggings as needed
Shirts as needed
Face painting
In south tattoos of animals on body
Headdresses
War bonnets
Eagle feathers
Buffalo horns
Buffalo robes in winter
Boots made from buffalo in winter

CHILDREN'S CLOTHING:
Children wore breechclouts and girls wore dresses after puberty, boys sometimes naked. Buffalo calf hides were used to wrap babies.

Buffalo hair stuffed into cradleboards.
Apache used soft fawn skins and rabbitskin bedding for babies, and used soft shredded cedar bark for diapers.

HAIR:
Their hair was often parted in the middle and the part was painted red. Northern men and women usually braided their hair into two braids, while southern tribes let their hair hang loose on their shoulders and back.

Men liked to tie charms in their hair and considered it aesthetic. Married Osage and Kansas women let their hair hang behind their backs while unmarried women's hair hung in front of their breasts. Blackfoot men wore their hair long and loose in the back with a narrow lock hanging over the nose and cut off square at the

Figure 7. *Boys war shirt made from antelope buckskin, Standing Rock Sioux. This shirt dates from about 1885-1900, it is the old style with open sides, however the rest of the shirt was sewn. The beaded strips on the sleeves and shoulders are probably from an older and perhaps larger shirt, recycled to fit. This shirt shows signs of much wear, and the stains at the neck and sleeves indicate a certain amount of sweating. This shirt is part of the collection that included the leggings (Figure 8.) Jack Stewart collection.*

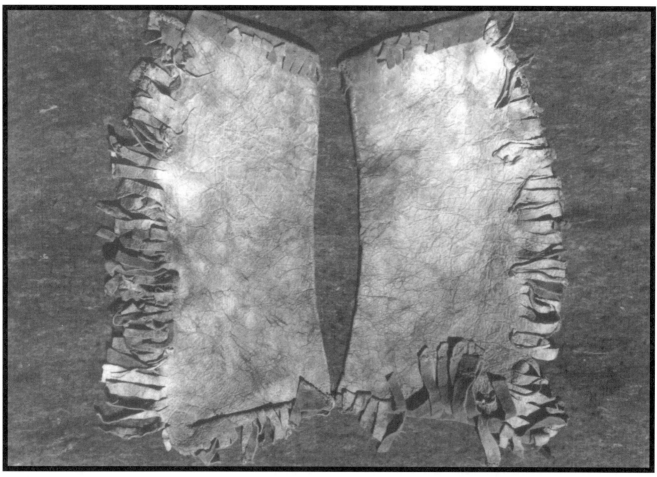

Figure 8. *Boys leggings from buffalo buckskin, Standing Rock Sioux, from about 1885-1900. These leggings were probably recycled from a mans shirt or leggings years before. The last buffalo hunts by these people were in 1883 and 1884. According to Jack Stewart, from the appearance of these leggings and the red ochre stain on them used in that time period, they would likely date to the late 1800's. Jack Stewart collection.*

end.

DECORATIONS:

Tattoos, paint, finger rings, bracelets, necklaces of shell, bone, and elk teeth, grizzly teeth and pendants. Feathers were personal decoration and the most prized were the black tipped white eagle feathers.

Tattoos and paint: Catlin painted pictures of many of the Plains Indians and showed face paint and tattoos in many of his paintings. He said that the neck, arms and breast were tattooed by pricking the skin and rubbing gunpowder and vermilion in the wounds. His paintings show women with tattoo lines on the chin, concentric circles on the cheeks, geometric designs on the neck and arms, circles and lines on arms and shoulders and concentric circles on the breasts around the nipples.

Catlin also illustrated young women with tattoos on the shoulders and across the top of the chest that looked like necklaces. The tattoo had lines running from one shoulder across the neckline to the other shoulder, and from these lines vees were drawn down on the chest that appear to represent claws, teeth or some other ornament. Comanche occasionally tattooed their faces and breasts. Wichita women painted or tattooed their breasts. Comanche women painted their ears and face.

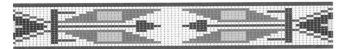

When thinking of Indian clothing many think of the full buckskin clothing with the fringe, quills, beads and feathers that the Plains Indians are known and popularized for in the movies. John Terrell in his book American Indian Almanac said it best: "The Dakota of the Northern Great Plains always have been, and always will be, the 'picture Indian' of Western History. They fully deserve the honor. For they rank physically, mentally, and morally among the highest type of American aborigines..."

George Catlin said "These people dress, not only with clothes comfortable for any latitude, but that they dress with some considerable taste and elegance."

Crow women were extremely skilled in making clothing and buckskin goods and the dressing of bighorn sheep.

Washington Irving toured the prairies in the 1800's and said the Osages were the finest Indians he had ever seen in the west. He said they were bare armed and bare chested and wore blankets around their loins with moccasins and leggings. He said their hair was shaved except for a crest on top and a long scalp lock in back. John D. Hunter speaking of the same Indians said that in warm weather both men and women wore breechclouts, moccasins and leggings.

Thomas E Mails described the plains clothing as being "mobile" in that as a person moved the fringe and dangling parts created unique light and shadow patterns while the beads, belts and bells scraped and jingled producing distinctive sounds.

It has been said that the tanned garments of the Plains people were far superior to all others. Many groups were known for their finely tanned and elegant clothing, but not all Plains groups took as much interest in their clothing. Pere Jacques Marquette apparently was the first to meet the Quapaw on the Arkansas River. He said the men have short hair and go naked and the women do not ornament themselves and dress in "wretched Skins." Perhaps he did not appreciate fine buckskin or possibly the appearance of people dressed in skins was unpleasant to him!

In primitive times the dress of the Plains Indians probably ranged from little clothing to full buckskins. Everyday work clothing for some groups was simple and crude and much simpler than their dress clothing. In early times their garments were tied together at the seams, and undecorated except for fringe along the edges of the garment.

Deer and elk skins were considered more serviceable for clothing for every day use. Antelope or mountain sheep was used to make their finest clothing. I suspect that deer and elk were more abundant so their hides naturally were used for everyday clothing. Antelope and mountain sheep possibly were less abundant or harder to get which may be partly why they were prized for finer dress clothing. Also antelope and bighorn sheep hides being comparatively thin tan very soft and supple and are excellent for clothing. And finally mountain sheep hides were often made into the classic two-skin dress with the decorative tail and hair fringe on the yoke. (See clothing description section for more details on two-skin dresses.)

Men's Clothing: In some areas during warm weather the men went naked but their usual clothing was undecorated breechclouts and soft soled moccasins and paint. The Blackfoot dyed their moccasins black. Although the breechclout was pretty much a universal article of clothing, it appears that some Plains groups, including the Blackfoot, did not wear them in early times but adopted them later. The Blackfoot wore leggings that apparently had flaps crossing over in front but left the buttocks bare.

Hip length leggings and shirts were added as needed for the weather. However in early times shirts were worn only rarely by men, but were worn occasionally to protect them in winter or from sunburn.

Shirts were made by sewing two skins together and were not decorated for everyday use. A few wore poncho like shirts. Face painting was common and in the south the men tattooed their thighs and other parts of their bodies with figures of animals.

In the winter men wore buffalo robes to protect them from the cold. Teton men were equipped for the worst of weather with a buffalo robe, their moccasins and a breechcloth.

They also used headdresses, war bonnets and eagle feathers, buffalo horns etc. The Crow had good physiques and loved elegant dress and long hair; they sometimes attached strands of hair long enough to reach the ground. Mandan men put glue and red earth into their hair and divided it into long flat slabs about two inches wide, it remained in this condition year round. It often hung below the waist and sometimes to the ground.

Face paint was common and several colors were used but red was their favorite.

Women's Clothing: Early dress for women in the Northern Plains appears to be a wrap around skirt. Later they adopted the strap dress, sometimes known as the slip and sleeve dress since it had shoulder straps and looked similar to a modern woman's slip. It had separate sleeves that could be attached or taken off according to the need. By the time Lewis and Clark visited the Upper Missouri River area in 1804 the Northern Plains women had abandoned the strap dress and were wearing the side fold dress. Within another forty years fashion had changed and by 1844 the transition from the side fold dress to the T-dress also called two-skin dress had been made. Abundant large game on the Northern Plains made it possible for the two-skin dresses to made and become the standard dress of the period. Two-skin buckskin dresses were worn into the reservation period when they began wearing cloth dresses.

They also added moccasins and knee length leggings when needed.

For winter wear, the hair was left on the skins to be worn next to the body for extra warmth. This may have been an influence from the Subarctic peoples, who also wear clothing made from hides with hair on the inside next to their skin. Buffalo robes were also added in the winter. Winter wear for the Comanche women was knee length leggings and a knee length dress.

The women in the Southern Plains wore

Figure 9. Girls dress from deer buckskin, Standing Rock Sioux, from about 1920-1935. While this is not an extremely old article, it is almost "classic" in the cut of the dress. The hides for this dress appear to be "wet-scraped" and the dress is a three skin style. Theodore Roosevelt Medora Foundation, Museum of the Badlands collection.

wrap around skirts or skirts that were two pieces of hide sewn together with thongs and were heavily fringed. There is evidence that some women may have wore breechclouts as well. Sometimes poncho like upper garments were added over the skirts and this evolved into the three-skin dress when they started lacing the top to the skirt. In the Southern Plains large game was less abundant than in the Northern Plains and with the smaller game (antelope and white tail deer) it usually required three skins to complete a dress. So while the two-skin dress became standard in the north the three-skin dress became common in the Southern Plains. By 1845, three-skin dresses had been adopted in the Southern Plains and were worn into the reservation period.

It was common in some areas for Plains women to paint and tattoo their faces, foreheads and breasts. They usually wore their hair long and loose or it was braided into two braids and they painted the part in their hair red. Assiniboine women prized long hair and some-times twisted in false hair to lengthen it.

In cold weather both men and women added buffalo robes, blankets, and boots made from buffalo hide.

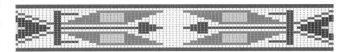

Bear grease was used by some groups as an insect repellent, it was rubbed on their bodies after bathing.

Although a limited practice, some Kansas and Osage women would wear stays to support their breasts during nursing.

Buffalo hair was used as stuffing for gloves pillows and other objects.

Plains dress clothing will be discussed briefly in the chapter describing selected traditional clothing. The reader should consult other sources if they are interested in more specific details. There are a number of good publications that cover Native American dress clothing.

THE SOUTHWEST

The Southwest Cultural area is mainly the states of Arizona and New Mexico, with a very small part of the surrounding states and extends south into Mexico. This is an arid but diverse land. It has low deserts and high mountains up to 12,000 feet. The area is sandy and has many mesas, cliffs, and strange rock formations all with many different colors. The temperature varies greatly and the area receives little rainfall, but it can be in the form of sudden violent thunderstorms, leaving washes everywhere. The few rivers are the Rio Grande, the Colorado, Pecos, Gila and Salt. Two principal lifestyles developed in the Southwest: One group was peaceful villagers who made their living farming and the other group was nomadic warriors who preyed on the villagers.

MEN'S CLOTHING:
Sandals
G-strings
Fiber or skin breechclouts
Cotton kilts
Buckskin shirts
Leggings in winter
Cotton breeches
Rabbit skin blankets
Cotton or wool woven blankets
Chin tattoos
Shells and beads

WOMEN'S CLOTHING:
Sandals
Small woven fiber aprons
Skirts or double aprons of twisted cords
Skin skirts

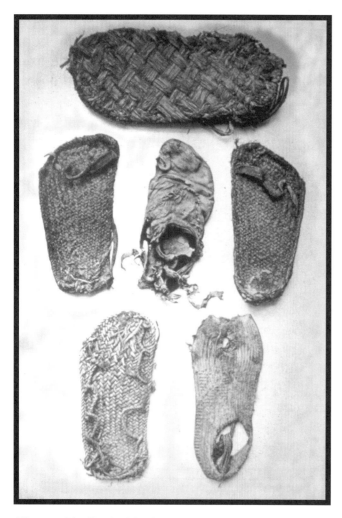

Figure 10. *Probably the single most important item of clothing for the Basketmakers and Anasazi in the Four Corners areas was the sandal. This collection of sandals and skin moccasin (center) was taken from Basketmaker III sites (a time period from about 550 - 750 AD) near Mesa Verde National Park in Northwestern Colorado. The sandals were made from Yucca fiber cords and show variation in construction from course woven elements to tightly woven from cords. Also shown is variation in the way the sandals were attached to the foot. The two center ones appear to have buckskin thongs that toes were slipped into and probably had cords used to tie the back of the sandal to the foot. The bottom left sandal has loops of cordage on the edges into which other cords were probably laced to hold it on. Photo courtesy of Mesa Verde National Park, The National Park Service.*

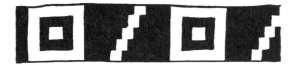

Apache Navaho and others:
Two piece or wrap skirts of cotton or deerskin
Poncho style tops
Long skin dresses
Navaho and Pueblo two-blanket dresses from cotton or wool with a long sash
Leggings in winter
Rabbit skin and turkey feather blankets
Chin tattoos
Shells and beads

CHILDREN'S CLOTHING:
Pecos Pueblo children and unmarried girls went nude. Havisupi children went naked until about six or seven years old then they wore full dress.

HAIR:
Early Basketmaker men had long hair tied in three lengths, but since women used human hair for many everyday items theirs was usually cropped.

In other areas both sexes probably had long hair. Mohaves liked glossy hair and rubbed it with mud and boiled mesquite bark. Pima men filled their hair with mud and formed it into a helmet and let it dry.

Unmarried Hopi women wore their hair in two large buns representing squash blossoms. After marriage the hair was wrapped with cords and tied into two pendant clubs which hung down the sides of the head representing squash fruits.

DECORATIONS:
Several items of decoration were used including bracelets, necklaces, pendants, ear pendants, buttons, rings, turquoise beads and shell beads brought in by trade from the Pacific. Body and face paint was used for ceremonial occasions, red paint being most common.

Yavapai painted their bodies with red clay to protect them from sun and for decoration. Faces were tattooed using cactus spines and charcoal.

Mohave men painted lines on legs, arms and chest. Mohave women also painted vertical stripes on their torso, breasts and arms. They painted their faces and blue marks were tattooed on the chins of married women. Both Mohave men and women liked to wear necklaces of wampum.

The Southwest Indians, when first discovered, were wearing garments of cotton which they grew and processed into cloth. Cabez de Vaca in his "Relacion" says that he found natives wearing linen and wool clothing. Other explorers said they encountered natives of Cibola wearing ankle length gowns.

Little is known about the clothing of the early inhabitants of the Four Corners area. These were the Basketmakers, the Anasazi (Cliff Dwellers) and the Pueblo. In hot areas the people probably wore little or no clothing. But it is known that sandals were the single most important item of clothing worn, to protect their feet from the rocky terrain. Hundreds of sandals and fragments have been found in Basketmaker sites.

Sandals were woven in several ways from yucca and other fibers. Some were made with different patterns on the top and bottom. Sandals found with knots on the underside may have provided traction on wet surfaces. Footwear also included moccasins.

Woven or twisted fibers were the main materials used for making clothing but animal skins were also used. In several areas women made skirts or double aprons from fibers that were

Figure 11. *Basketmaker apron made from yucca fiber cords. The waist band appears to be twine woven and corded yucca fibers are attached and hang from the bottom of the waist band. This woman's apron was taken from a Basketmaker III site (550-750 AD) near Mesa Verde National Park. Photo courtesy of Mesa Verde National Park, The National Park Service.*

shredded or twisted into cords. Yucca fibers, juniper bark, and the inner bark of willow and cottonwood were commonly used.

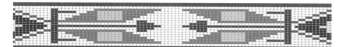

Apache, Navaho and other women wore deerskin and cotton two piece or wrap skirts, poncho style tops and long skin dresses. Navaho women also wore dresses made from two blankets attached together at the shoulders and sides and were held with a belt. Pueblo women wore a similar dress made from cotton or wool attached over the right shoulder but leaving the left shoulder bare. Early Pueblo women wore cotton aprons. The only clothing worn by some Zuni women were very small cotton aprons with minimal coverage secured with a cord around the waist.

In the Four Corners area the Basketmaker and Anasazi men wore fiber sandals and G-strings or possibly breechclouts. The main clothing for other Southwest men appears to have been fiber or skin breechclouts, although in pre-Spanish days men sometimes wore cotton kilts, cotton poncho tops, breeches and buckskin shirts. Pueblo men wore a white cotton kilt held around the waist with a colorful sash.

Leggings were worn by both men and women when needed. In winter blankets were used that were made from rabbit skin, turkey feathers and buffalo hides or they were woven from wool, cotton or yucca. Adornment included chin tattooing, shell beads, headdresses of yucca and other decorations.

Young Zuni women were required to go entirely naked until they married. A young man wove a blanket and presented it to the girl he wished to marry, she put it on and became his wife. Pecos Pueblo young women also went nude until marriage.

It appears that most Southwest rectangle or blanket dresses were tied or sewn over the right shoulder leaving the left arm and shoulder out. The Zuni appear to be the exception by wear-

Figure 12. *Basketmaker period woven yucca apron. This apron is about 5 1/2 inches wide and about 32 inches long and consists of approximately 240 two-ply yucca fiber strings hanging from a woven area at the top. The woven band, with a red, black, yellow and white design appears to be a plain weave; over and under. These aprons were suspended from a cord (sometimes made from human hair) that was tied around the waist and the hanging strings were tucked between the legs and looped over the waist cord in the back. This apron was collected from a cave in Northeastern Arizona and was on display at Mesa Verde National Park for a number of years and then returned to the American Museum of Natural History in New York. Photo courtesy of Mesa Verde National Park, The National Park Service.*

ing their dresses tied over the left shoulder and leaving the right shoulder and arm out. Coronado on reaching the Seven Cities of Cibol (Zuni) in 1540 found natives wearing cotton blankets. He said the women tie them over the left shoulder leaving the right arm out.

This type of dress apparently was worn quite loose. A painting by Richard H. Kerns done in 1851 of Yampai Indians near the Zuni shows the blanket dress over the left shoulder and leaving the right arm, shoulder and breast bare. Other artists have depicted the same style of loose clothing for the Anasazi showing the dresses attached over the right shoulder leaving the left arm, shoulder and breast exposed.

THE BASIN AND PLATEAU

The Great Basin cultural area lies west of the Rocky Mountains and extends to the Sierra Nevada Mountains to the west. It is composed mainly of Nevada and Utah and has parts of Colorado, Wyoming, Idaho, Oregon and California in it. The central portion of the basin has no drainage to the oceans and is arid with bitter cold winters and hot summers. The Basin has sparse vegetation and has vast plains, desserts, mountains and salty lakes.

To the early explorers and pioneers the Great Basin was a dreaded desert that had to be crossed to reach California and Oregon. But everywhere they went they met Indians and marveled how they could exist in such a vast wasteland. They were also appalled by these natives who they saw traveling around nearly naked. Lewis and Clark and other explorers reported seeing Indians traveling in winter, barefoot over snow and ice and only wearing breechclouts. They said their feet were hardened almost like hooves.

WOMEN'S CLOTHING:
Single or double aprons
Fiber aprons
Buckskin aprons
Basketry hats
Fiber sandals
Skirts and blouses woven from pounded bark
Skirts of bark, grass or skin
Rabbit skin and feather robes
Sleeveless tunics
Plains style clothing in later times

Figure 13. Sagebrush bark skirt and top. This artifact was found in northern Nevada and is modeled by Genevive Olivas. This skirt and top are from the collections of the Jerry Lee Young Idaho Heritage Museum, Hollister. Skirts, tops and other items were twine woven by the Basin and Plateau groups using sagebrush bark and other fibers. A detailed description is in the chapter on making traditional clothing.

Shell beads
Chin tattooing

MEN'S CLOTHING:
Skin and fiber breechclouts
Fiber sandals
Hard soled moccasins (some groups)
Shirts and pants from pounded bark
Rabbit skin and feather robes
Skin shirts
Skin leggings

CHILDREN'S CLOTHING:
Babies were wrapped in jackrabbit, deerskins and wildcat skins. Diapers were made from shredded tules. Cradleboards were made from chokecherry and other supple twigs. Soft tanned antelope skins were used for cradleboard covers.

Plateau children dressed similar to adults. Boys went nude in warm weather but also used breechclouts, leggings, poncho style skins and small robes. Small girls dressed in dresses made from two fawn skins with hair attached, they were sewn across the shoulders and laced here and there on the sides.

Western Shoshone children went nude in summer, but some girls wore front aprons.

FOOTWEAR:
Footwear ranged from crude twine woven sandals to moccasins made from deer and elk skin, also going barefoot was common.

HAIR:
Usually long and loose, feathers were tied to hair, the hair part was often painted and they used headbands of buckskin, rabbit skin or duck skin.

DECORATIONS:
Body and face tattooing, painting (usually red but also white, yellow and black) and ear pierc-

ing were all common forms of decoration. A few important men sometimes pierced the nasal septum and wore a stick or bone in it. Tattoos were made by rubbing grease and soot on the skin and pricking the design into the skin with a thorn. Three vertical lines on the chin was probably the most common tattoo. Utes painted dark circles on cheeks and white circles on forehead. Paiutes used strings of beads for decoration.

Grease and red ocher were rubbed on skin to soften it and protect it from the sun and wind.

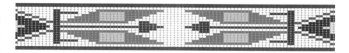

It is thought that clothing changed very little in the Basin for thousands of years. The usual clothing for women was a short double or single apron or skirt and for men it was nothing. Clothing seemed to be an unnecessary burden. In some areas in the summer heat, shade was needed more than clothing and the people would wear as little clothing as possible.

But clothing was worn for decoration or ceremonial purposes and for protection against severe weather and the many thorns and sharp twigs.

Although the men went entirely without clothing at times, women may not have, at least in some areas, since there was an old taboo that anyone looking at an entirely naked woman would go blind.

The women's aprons were usually made of fibers such as pounded or shredded juniper or sagebrush bark, yucca, dogbane or other fibers and fur (rabbit skin). They twisted the fibers into cordage and looped them over a belt of fibers or human hair. One such string apron found was about 12 inches long and a little less in width. Small buckskin aprons have also been reported. Pounded sage and juniper bark was woven into skirts and blouses. In addition to the aprons the women wore basketry hats, yucca sandals and shell beads. Chin tattooing was common. In later times sleeveless tunics were worn and some adopted Plains style dresses including long two-skin dresses for winter. Kwaiisu women usually went bare breasted and wore either a breechcloth or a two piece skirt.

As mentioned Basin men's clothing was scanty, but fiber, skin and fur breechclouts and fiber sandals (sage or tule) have been reported. Later they used skin shirts and leggings.

Rabbit robes or blankets were considered by some as the greatest luxury in the basin. Also if one was lucky enough to have a buffalo robe, the owner was considered rich. Robes were also made from elk, deer, marmot, ground squirrel, beaver, coyote, lynx and other fur animals. Even though early clothing in the Basin and Plateau was scanty, it was much finer in later years. Following the influence of the Plains Indians the Basin and Plateau peoples began dressing in Plains style clothing. The buckskin tanned by the Utes was considered to be exceptionally well done. And it was reported in 1776 by Val'ez de Escalante that "The Eastern Ute had surplus deerskins to trade."

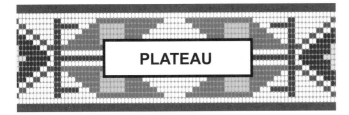

PLATEAU

The Columbia Plateau consists of parts of the states of Oregon, Washington, Idaho and Montana and extends north into British Columbia. This area contains sagebrush deserts, high plains, some marsh areas and mountain valleys with pine and fir trees being predominant. The two main rivers that drain the area are the Columbia on the south and the Fraser in the north. These two rivers are fed by many tributaries and the network of rivers provided the natives with salmon, trout and sturgeon.

Plateau clothing was similar to Basin clothing. However big game was more plentiful in the Plateau and the people could obtain more hides

for use in making clothing. Clothing was made from deer, antelope, elk and other skins with the hair on or off. Both sexes of the Northern Shoshone and Bannock wore breechclouts. Leggings and moccasins were used in the Plateau and winter robes were made from rabbit skin, buffalo and sometimes mudhen feathers. Rabbitskin blankets were the basic item of clothing and were used for both clothing and bedding. Tule capes and animal pelts were used for rain gear.

The women wore small front and back aprons, footwear similar to socks made from sage and juniper bark and fez (conical) shaped basketry hats. Later they wore fringed skin tunics with a belt.

Plateau men wore nothing or just rabbit skin robes, but later used full buckskin clothing including skin caps.

The Washo wore clothing made from well-tanned deerskins, rabbits, fox, wolves and coyotes. The Nez Perce seemed to wear full buckskins daily including breechclout, leggings, moccasins, and blanket for the men and full Plains style dresses for the women. Coeur d'Alene men wore a small poncho top in winter over their shirt.

Figure 14. *The Western Shoshone made a headdress similar to a bill cap or sun visor from rawhide, it had a buckskin thong to tie under the chin. They also made skin snow goggles from rawhide to protect their eyes from the bright light. They were shaped similar to modern glasses with a small slit to look through.*

The Paiutes made clothing from sagebrush and other fibers. Some of which were fiber mats that hung down in front and back with a hole in the center for the neck; they were tied on the sides but had no sleeves. They also made sagebrush or cattail mats that were draped around the shoulders or wrapped around the waist.

Paiute women wore basketry hats which protected their heads from pine pitch when gathering pine nuts and from tumplines when they were carrying a load.

Footwear: Sandals were common footwear, many have been found in caves in the Great Basin. They were made from fibers such as sagebrush bark, yucca and tules. Tules were used frequently because they were easy to prepare, but the tule sandals didn't last as long as those made from sagebrush bark.

A unique practice in footwear used by the Basin people was to smear pitch on the bottom of their feet for protection. The Kawaiisu had a similar practice in that they would reinforce their moccasins for travel by smearing pinion pitch on the soles and then stomp in ashes. (I presume this would also give the soles more traction, help them wear better and probably waterproofed them as well).

Cold weather shoes were twined from heavy cord and stuffed with pounded sagebrush bark. Northern Paiutes made rabbit skin socks to wear under their twined sagebrush bark moccasins in the winter. Southern Paiutes made twined bark leggings for winter wear. Sometimes leggings were made by just wrapping hides around the legs.

"Foot mittens" were made from squirrel or badger skins and in summer rawhide sandals were used.

Moccasins were made from animal skins and coarsely woven bark. Badger skin was preferred for moccasins.

THE CALIFORNIA

The California cultural area comprises most of the state of California except for parts of the southeastern portion of the state. The cultural area to the south includes Baja California in Mexico, and the northern boundary is arbitrarily drawn more or less at the Oregon-California border, but the northern Californians had many similarities in culture to the natives of the northwest coast.

The northern part of the area is forested with tall trees, many rivers and a rocky coastline. The central part of the area is a huge fertile valley with mountains to the east and the sea coast to the west. The southern portion is mountainous and arid.

The people in the California cultural area foraged in the higher elevations in the summer and moved to lower elevations in the winter. There was an ample food supply in this region. There were a variety of plant foods available with acorns being a staple and plentiful fish, deer and other small game.

MEN'S CLOTHING:
Some areas no clothing
Bark or skin breechclouts
Fiber sandals
Skin moccasins
Sea otter furs
Headbands with feathers
Rabbitskin robes
Feather blankets
Full body tattoos

WOMEN'S CLOTHING:
Some areas no clothing
Front and back aprons

Figure 15. *California man and woman. Drawing by Cheryl Vierstra*

Fiber sandals
Skin moccasins
Basketry caps
Rabbit skin blankets
Feather blankets

CHILDREN'S CLOTHING:
Young children, no clothing
Older children dressed like the adults
Diapers made from mesquite bark

HAIR:
Usually long, sometimes to the shoulders in both sexes. Hair was cut with a piece of burning wood or a sharp obsidian flake. Some men tied their hair in two bunches, others braided it and tied it up on the head and some wore string hair nets. Some cut it to 4 or 5 inches long. Southeastern Pomo men wore long hair and used a sling as a head band, where it was instantly available when needed. Various types of head bands and netted caps were also used to hold hair. Miwok men and women braided their hair.

Women's hair was worn short or long, sometimes with bangs leaving the rest long or tied up into two rolls with thongs.

Women put clay on their heads, let it dry and then broke it off to get rid of parasites and to keep the hair glossy.

DECORATIONS:
Women: Tattoos on forehead, face, chin and breasts

Both sexes had straight lines tattooed from the chin to the navel. A water color painting done by Louis Choris in 1816, shows straight lines tattooed on a woman's chin and zig zag lines from the corners of her mouth down to the chin. Another shows straight lines on the chin and neck and a double line going straight down from the neck to the navel. This same woman has several rows of zig zag lines around the neck, on the chest, shoulders and around the upper arms. Young girls were tattooed with three lines on their chin so they would not look like men.

Men had vertical lines tattooed on the chin and nose and also tattooed arms, chest and abdomen. Some had vertical and horizontal lines tattooed on their foreheads. Some Southern California men had full body tattoos.

Face and body paint was made by mixing grease with pigments which were usually red and white clay, red stone, charcoal, and a fungus from a fir tree.

Necklaces were made from juniper berries, nuts, beads, olivella shells, clam shells, bear claws, dentalium and magnesite cylinders.

Women pierced their ears and wore feather or bone ornaments in them. They also pierced the nasal septum. Men also pierced the nasal septums and wore feathers in them.

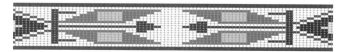

Northwest California clothing, depending on the weather, was usually scant and sometimes no clothing was worn by both sexes.

The usual clothing for the California women was front and back aprons. Sometimes it was just a front apron. The front one was made from cotton or other plant fibers twisted into cordage or sometimes it was made from fringed buckskin or deer fur. The back apron could be made from buckskin but was often made from shredded willow bark and in some areas it was large and bustle like. Southern California women wore grass skirts. Beads were commonly used on fringed skirts as a decoration. Women also wore breechclouts. The southeastern Pomo women wore large breechclouts made from buckskin or rabbit skin, but tule skirts were their usual attire. Wealthy Yana women wore belts of human hair and skirts with leather tassels braided with grass. These skirts sometimes had pine nut beads strung on them. Certain women's cordage skirts had asphalt balls on the ends of the fibers, reported to have kept their skirts from blowing in the wind, but they may have been just for decoration.

Basketry caps were also worn. The caps protected their heads from the carrying strap of their burden baskets.

California men often wore no clothes, but would wear skin or bark breechclouts or a piece of skin wrapped around the waist. Fur skirts were also reported for men. Men's footwear was the same as women's but was rarely worn. Some men had sea otter furs, headbands with feathers, and full body tattoos.

Both men and women used rabbit skin robes and feather blankets as needed. Blankets were worn in the daytime as clothing and used at night as bedding. Blankets were made from rabbit, puma, wildcat, sea otter, bear, deer, fox and even gopher skins. These were made by either sewing skins together or by weaving twisted strips of skin together. Tule and buckskin leggings were worn as needed by both men and women. In cool weather mud was sometimes used to cover their bodies to keep them warm. Fur and feather caps as well as snow shoes were used by Californians. Also in winter they stuffed their moccasins and leggings with grass or wore leggings made from skins with the hair side in. For protection from the rain they made mantles from shredded tules or the inner bark of willow and redwood. These were tied around the neck.

Footwear was crudely made and included skin or fiber moccasins, agave fiber sandals and tule leggings.

Californians usually went barefooted around the village but wore moccasins and leggings on food gathering and hunting trips. Both men and women wrapped buckskin around the lower legs to protect them from rattlesnakes.

Sandals were made of woven fibers wrapped around a looped frame. In some the soles were made an inch thick to protect their feet from the hot ground. Moccasins and leggings were twine woven from tules, or made from deerskin. Pitch was often smeared on soles of the buckskin moccasins. In protective gear the Californians made armored vests from split branches that were woven tightly together with hemp.

THE NORTHWEST COAST

The Northwest Coast cultural area is a narrow strip of land along the coast from about the Oregon-California border to the Yakutat Bay in Southeast Alaska. The area has a mild climate with heavy rainfall creating a true rain forest. The predominant species of trees are cedar and hemlock. There are thousands of islands and fjords along the coastline. Numerous streams and rivers running to the sea are fed from melting glaciers to the east. The culture had no agriculture but the sea and forest supplied the people with abundant food and shelter.

WOMEN'S CLOTHING:
Skin or fiber skirts
Front and back aprons of skin or fiber
Fiber sleeveless jackets
Conical rain caps
Skin robes

MEN'S CLOTHING:
Skin robes
Feather robes
Breechclouts
Aprons

Figure 16. *Northeast Coast Man and Woman. Drawing by Cheryl Vierstra*

Leggings
Moccasins
Fur hats
Fiber basketry hats
Fiber rain caps

CHILDREN'S CLOTHING:

Children dressed similar to the adults. Cedar bark pounded soft was used as a lining for baby cradles. Diapers were woven from cedar bark.

HAIR:

Men wore their hair long, it was left loose, braided or tied in one bunch and coated with grease from bear or deer. Some men allowed their facial hair to grow. Women parted their hair in the middle, wore two braids and painted the part red.

DECORATIONS:

Women tattooed their chins, arms, legs, chest and breasts. Both sexes painted their faces and wore earrings, nose ornaments, necklaces, finger rings, copper bracelets and anklets. In some groups men tattooed one arm to measure strings of dentalium. Bodies and faces were painted as a protection against sunburn.

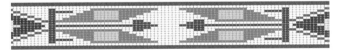

The Northwest peoples were conditioned to the cool moist air and many people went nearly naked most of the year. In good weather men sometimes wore only ornaments, but they also wore skin breechclouts, aprons, leggings, moccasins, and fur or fiber hats and tule rain caps. When weather demanded they used robes made from feathers, deerskin, bearskin and other furs.

Northwest coast women wore skirts or front and back aprons made from skins, goat wool, shredded cedar bark and other fibers. In the south the fiber skirts were decorated with seeds on the front and shells on the back below the hips. Usually just the front apron was worn around the house.

Deerskin breechclouts were also worn by women. Sometimes women wore sleeveless jackets made from goat wool or other fibers. Dress clothing was tunics of woven cedar bark. Short buckskin leggings, and conical rain caps were used and skin robes were added as needed. Chin tattooing was practiced in some areas. Shredded cedar bark aprons were suspended with a cedar bark belt.

Disposable cattail or reed skirts were made as work clothing to be worn while they were butchering seals or whales brought to shore by the men.

The Northwest Coast peoples made specialized rain gear to shed water in the moist climate in which they lived. Conical hats were made from spruce roots, cedar bark or tules and were sometimes double layered to more effectively shed the rain. Water shedding rain capes were also made from fur or woven cedar bark and other fibers. In cold weather a second robe woven of shredded yellow cedar bark was worn under the rain cape.

Blankets and robes were made from woven mountain goat wool, cedar bark, bearskin, dog hair, feathers and even small mammals such as marmots and ground squirrels. Robes were also made from sea mammals including sea otter, sea lion, and others. It was considered taboo to sew a robe that contained both sea mammal skins and land mammal skins.

The people went barefoot most of the time even in the snow, however they would also make moccasins and wore them in cold weather. Rich men had sealskin or bearskin moccasins, others would wrap their feet with cedar bark matting. Both sexes usually wore leggings and dressed hides for cold weather. Leggings were

made from woven cedar bark and would protect them from brush when traveling.

Farther north more clothing was needed and the people dressed similar to the Eskimos with their boots pants and mittens. Tlingit wore buckskin shirts and pants with moccasins attached.

Tlingit women wore a buckskin slip under their skirts in cold weather. In the summer shirts were worn with the hair inside and in the winter a hooded shirt was added. Gut skin water shedding parkas with hoods were worn in wet weather.

THE ARCTIC AND SUBARCTIC

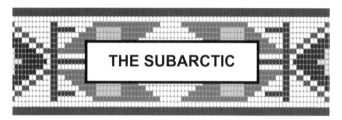

THE SUBARCTIC

The Subarctic cultural area contains much of Canada and Alaska. The northern border is the tree line where the Eskimo world begins. This diverse area contains large plains, coniferous forests, high mountain peaks, tundra to the north, many rivers, streams, lakes and swamplands and has abundant animals, fish and birds. Much of this area is known as the Northern Forest and contains primarily pine, spruce and fir but also has birch, aspen and willow. The area has short summers followed by long harsh winters. The people were primarily nomadic fishers and hunters and depended in a large part on the caribou and other large game and fur species for their sustenance. The fur was as important to them for clothing as the meat was for food. Birch bark was an important material for making canoes and many containers.

MEN'S CLOTHING:
Pants with moccasins attached
Hide shirts with long tails

WOMEN'S CLOTHING:
Hide shirts with long tails and hoods
Mittens hanging on strings through the shirt sleeves
Pants with moccasins attached

CHILDREN'S CLOTHING:
Children dressed similar to adults.

Figure 17. Bering Coast Eskimo woman and child. Photo courtesy of Anchorage Museum of History and Art. Photo # B82.46.86

BABIES:
Fur lined bags
Bark lined cradles
Clothing made from hare skin
Disposable diapers were made from sphagnum moss.
Babies were wrapped in soft hides from caribou embryos.

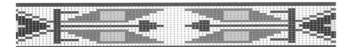

Men's and women's clothing was similar. It is reported that early aboriginals wore a one piece skin underwear of tanned caribou skin that went from the neck to mid calf. Dehaired shirts were worn in the summer and haired clothing was worn over these in the winter. The Subarctic peoples learned to make clothing from the Eskimos and in the north the clothing was similar to the Eskimo clothing. They had caribou parkas with the hair left on and moccasins of moose, caribou or water resistant seal skin. Pants and leggings were both made with moccasins attached. Their hide shirts were well fitted and tailored and had long front and back tails. Socks were made from hare skins or grass.

In winter two shirts were worn, the first or inner one with the hair against the body and the outside shirt having the hair to the outside. Women's shirts were a little longer than the men's and had hoods attached and mittens that hung through the sleeves on strings. Fur lined bags and bark lined cradles were made for babies.

Caribou hide was the major material used for making clothing but moose and elk were also used. The hair was removed and the skins were dressed and smoked and clothing sewn with sinew thread. Leggings, moccasins and robes with sleeves were made. Some robes had detachable sleeves. Other clothing material included beaver, lynx, hare, marmot, ground squirrels, gut, fish skins, bird skins and others. Some skins were not always tanned.

Fur skins were made into both parkas and blankets. Robes and blankets were used for both clothing and bedding.

Women wore short skin tunics made from moose or caribou hide, skin leggings, skin aprons and fur blankets. They had dresses that were cut like a mans shirt but longer and wore trousers with moccasins attached. Cree women wore long skin dresses and hooded cloaks. Dresses and skirts were made from caribou hide and were worn with the hair side out.

Men wore long skin breechclouts held with a belt, leggings that went to the thigh, a long skin shirt or tunic to the knee and moccasins. In winter another caribou or beaver tunic was added. A cloak or fur blanket was also worn. Some wore trousers with or without attached feet. They had socks of caribou with the hair turned to the inside, animal pelt hats and mittens. Garters and rabbit skin vests and short hide coats are also reported.

In 1613 David Pelletier made a drawing of a Subarctic man and woman apparently in the summertime. The women is shown in a short fringed skirt that ends several inches above the knee and a top that goes over the left shoulder but exposes the right shoulder and breast. The man wears a short kilt or skirt also several inches above the knee and has a decorative looking hat.

THE ARCTIC

This far north cultural area begins at the tree line in Canada and Alaska where the Subarctic cultural area ends. It is more than 5,000 miles wide from Greenland across Canada and Alaska to eastern Siberia. This is a land of dark and long bitter winters full of ice and snow and short lived summers. The main vegetation is mosses, lichens and scrub bush. The people, the Aleuts and Inuit (Eskimos) live primarily by hunting sea animals, caribou, moose and beaver.

MEN'S AND WOMEN'S CLOTHING:

Arctic clothing was basically the same for both men and women and consisted of:
Inner pants
Outer pants
Inner parka
Outer parka
Socks
Boots

CHILDREN'S:
Children's clothing was made from eider duck skins.
Absorbent ptarmigan feathers were used for diapers

HAIR:
Women parted their hair in the middle and braided it at the side. Men cut their hair short except for a two inch strip left long that went from the crown to the back of the head. Beads were worn on this strip.

DECORATIONS:
Women tattooed their faces and lower lips. Three lines were made from the lower lip to the chin. They tattooed their arms and thighs by stitching sooty thread through their skin. This was considered a sign of feminine beauty. Men wore labrets made from walrus ivory at each corner of the mouth. They also wore beads on their clothing and pendants or amulets on the neck.

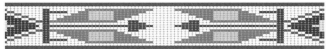

Eskimo clothing had to meet two requirements, it had to be warm and it had to be pliable so they could move. Men and women dressed similar. Their clothing was well made and tailored and would keep them warm in the bitterest cold weather. Eskimo women spent many hours sewing their families clothing but in addition they took the time to decorate it.

The Arctic peoples had six basic types of clothing: 1) An inner pullover parka worn hair side in, 2) Outer pullover parka worn hair side out, 3) inner pants worn hair side in, 4) Outer pants worn hair side out, 5) socks and 6) boots. There were many style variations of the above basic six pieces of clothing. For example they made at least 15 different types of boots each with a different name. Sealskin was used to make waterproof boots and other waterproof clothing which was worn during the wet season.

Clothing was made primarily from caribou skins because of its warmth and availability. But seal, polar bear, fox, dog, and bird skins were all used when caribou was scarce. They also used the hides from ground squirrels, hares and marmots, and the intestines from sea mammals. Boots were made from seal skin and caribou leg skin. Bedding was made from winter caribou skins and polar bear skins.

Usually the under clothing was worn with the hair turned inside next to the body and the outer clothing had the hair turned to the outside. During the summer the Eskimos would just wear their winter underwear but they would turn the hair side out.

In addition to the above the women made bird skin parkas and dress up parkas from ground squirrel skins. Women's parkas had two long narrow flaps, one in front and one in back and had large "pouches" or pockets. Their parkas were made large and had a pouch under the hood to accommodate packing their babies on their backs inside the parkas. The shoulders and arm holes were made large enough to allow them to bring the baby around to the front to nurse without having to take the baby out of the parka. These loose parkas could be drawn tight at the waist to eliminate updrafts of cold air.

In addition to the pants men wore shirts with-out hoods and to this they added parkas without hoods which had high collars. These high collars are thought to be the forerunners of hoods. They also wore fur hats, mittens and boots. Some men's parkas were made from eider duck skins. Their parkas had a short tail in back and a long one in front. Waterproof jackets or parkas were made from sea mammal intestines sewn together. These were worn over other clothing when kayaking. A similar one piece waterproof suit was made that had pants, boots, top and hood all in one piece.

An important item of clothing developed and worn by the Arctic peoples was snow goggles. These special goggles protected their eyes from the bright light and reflections off the snow. They were usually carved from wood or ivory and had small slits that restricted the amount of light that could go through them.

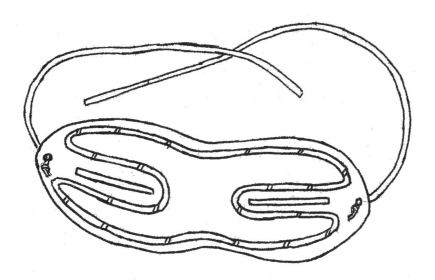

Figure 18. *Arctic snow goggles.*

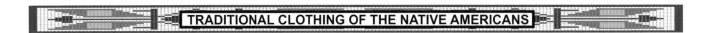

NOTES

DESCRIPTION OF SELECTED TRADITIONAL CLOTHING AND MAKING TRADITIONAL CLOTHING

This chapter describes in more detail some of the items of traditional clothing talked about in the first section of the book. In addition this chapter provides information and ideas for making replicas of traditional clothing either from buckskin or other materials.

APRONS AND SKIRTS

An apron is basically a piece of material with strings or straps to tie it on around the waist. The term apron generally refers to one piece that is worn only in the front of the body. However some groups wore double aprons, one worn in front and another in the back. The term apron is also used interchangeably with skirts. Even the single apron is sometimes called a skirt. Aprons were common wear for native women in the Southwest, Basin/Plateau, California and the Northwest Coast. Aprons are also reported for men in the Northwest Coast and possibly they were in limited use in other areas.

FIBER APRONS AND SKIRTS

Southwest Basketmaker women's early aprons were made of yucca strings or shredded juniper bark fibers hung from a cord tied around the waist. Yucca strings were later woven into small pieces of cloth about 2 or 3 inches wide and 5 or 6 inches long. This apron had a heavy fringe on the bottom from the warp threads that were left hanging. Some had woven or painted designs on them.

In the Great Basin, The Paiute women made aprons from a variety of materials. It has been said that if their husbands were lazy or not good hunters the women had to wear fiber skirts. The skirt (apron) was twined from grass, bark, tules or other fibers. Normally they extended to about mid thigh or a little longer. Usually just a front apron was worn with no covering behind. Single aprons that were held up with a belt were also made from buckskin, mudhen skins, rabbit skins, coyote and badger skins.

Southwest Basketmaker women made aprons

Figure 19. An apron which is similar to those made by the Southwest Basketmakers.

from yucca strings that were looped over a waist cord and then twined together for a short distance directly below the waist cord. The yucca strings then just hung loose from the waist cord.

Figure 19 is an apron made by the author which is similar in size to some Southwest basketmaker aprons. It is six inches wide and twelve inches long and is made from jute fiber. It is twined together at the top and the string used to twine the fibers together is also the waist cord.

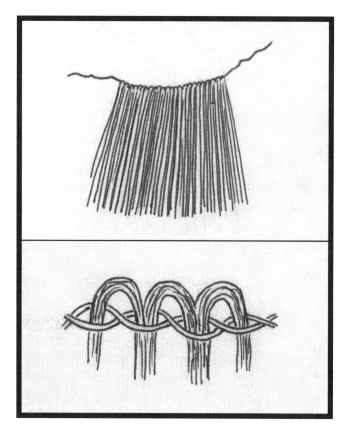

***Figure 20**. Detail of one Southwest method of twining a skirt.*

Willow bark skirts were made by Southwest Cocopa women. *Figure 20* shows how the bark strips were twined into the waist cord. Ethnology catalog number 209736 of the Smithsonian Institution Department of Anthropology is a willow bark skirt in their collection. This is the front part of a traditional front and back skirt made by the Cocopa Indians of lower California. This

skirt is made from willow bark strips folded in half and twined together at the fold with cordage. The cordage then formed the skirts belt.

To make a similar skirt collect bark strips twice as long as the desired length of the skirt or use jute cords. Then cut a jute cord long enough to go around the waist about two and a half or three times. Double the cord and begin twisting it into a two ply cord. After about a foot of two ply cord is made begin adding in bark strips. Just lay in a small bundle of fibers in between the two ply at the center of the fibers. Give the cord a twist around the fibers. Next fold the fiber bundle down, as illustrated, and lay in another bundle of fibers next to the first bundle. Twine twist the two cords around the fibers and again fold the fiber over and lay in another bundle. Proceed in this manner until the desired width of apron is achieved. Then continue to twist the two fibers into a two ply cord and tie a knot in the end. If desired make a second apron to complete the pair for a double apron.

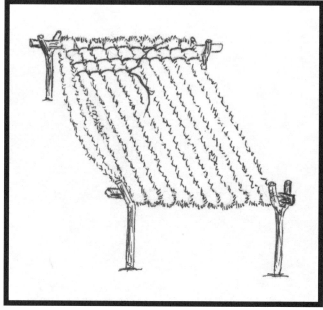

Figure 21. *Loom for making a mudhen skin skirt.*

Paiute women would make skirts from mudhen skins. The mudhen skins were cut into strips

40

and twisted into ropes. The skin and feather ropes were wrapped around two poles supported on forked sticks stuck in the ground like a horizontal loom. Fibers were then twine woven into the skins to form the skirt. It is thought that this formed a tubular skirt, the woman would step into it, pull it up and tie it on with strings attached to the top.

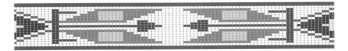

In 1875 a skirt was collected in California that was made from hundreds of strands of corded milkweed fibers. The fibers were looped over a waist band in bundles and twine woven together with several inches of twining from the waist band down. From the bottom of the twining the fibers then hung free. The bottom ends of the cords are knotted. This skirt is in the collections of the Department of Anthropology Smithsonian Institution catalog # 21377.

Figure 22. *Instead of bundles of milkweed, jute cord was used to make this skirt.*

Shown above, in *Figure 22*, is an apron or skirt made in a similar fashion from jute cords. To make this skirt cut a buckskin waist band about 1/2 inch wide and long enough to be tied around the waist. Then cut jute fibers about four feet long, these will be doubled over the waist band to make the skirt. Cut another jute fiber about six or eight feet long (weft) to be used in twining the skirt fibers together. Tie the waistband horizontally between two points, fold the skirt cords (warps) in half and loop them over the waist band. Then beginning with the skirt cords on the left, loop the weft around the first two cords and twist the weft cords around the warp in a counter clockwise direction one half turn. Then insert the next two warps and again twist the weft cords in the same manner, twine weaving them together.

Continue inserting warps and twining them together until the last warp is reached and the skirt is the desired width. At the last warp on the right just wrap both strands of the weft around it in opposite directions, turn the work around so that the last warp is now on the left and proceed as before twining the strands together working from left to right. When the weft strands are about used up, just loop a new one as before around the last warps that were twined and continue twining as before. The old weft strands can just hang down and become part of the warp strands.

Add as many rows of twining as desired and tie off the weft letting the free ends hang down with the warps. If desired tie the bottom ends with overhand knots to keep the ends from unraveling.

Another similar skirt is in the Department of Anthropology of the Smithsonian Institution catalog # 203595 and was collected in California in 1899. This skirt is made from strips of willow bark (*Salix nigna*) that appear to be looped over a waist cord and twined together with just a few rows of twining under the waist cord. The remainder of the bark strands hang free.

PLATEAU
A painting housed in the collections of the Tho-

Figure 23. *Modern sagebrush skirt.*

mas Gilcrease Institute of American History and Art shows Idaho Governor Caleb Lyon presenting a treaty to the local Indians in the spring of 1866. The clothing shown is probably dress clothing. Some of the women are depicted wearing cordage skirts. The skirts consist of waistbands with cords hanging loosely from them. Attached to each waistband is a row of feathers forming a decorative band around the waist.

SOUTHWEST

Mohave women wore a double apron or skirt. The front part was made from twisted fiber cords in various colors hanging from the girdle (cord) around the hips. The back part was a mass of strips of the inner bark of cottonwood, these were also tied to the cord around the waist.

SAGEBRUSH SKIRTS & OTHER CLOTHING

Figures 23 and *24* show a sagebrush skirt and blouse for a woman. Both these items are in the collections of the Idaho Museum of Natural History, Idaho State University Pocatello, ID. The blouse is Catalog #5596 and the skirt is #5597. Both were made by Mrs. Wuzzie George of Fallon Nevada and were purchased from her and placed in the museums collections. This skirt and blouse along with sagebrush bark pants and a shirt were made by Wuzzie in the early part of the twentieth century. Wuzzie and her husband Jimmy would sometimes wear this bark clothing in parades and for other exhibitions.

The blouse or *Sagwa Kwassy* the Paiute name, is authentic as to fabric but probably not as to pattern. Mrs. George believes the old people made sagebrush bark tops similar to hers but they did not have sleeves. They also were tied at the sides and probably not open in the front.

Figure 24. *Modern sagebrush blouse.*

42

(See old style (*Figure 27*) for comparison.)

There is also a mans shirt that looks essentially the same as the woman's blouse and a pair of sagebrush bark mans pants in the collection. This collection includes several three strand braided sagebrush bark belts that may have been used to tie around the waist while wearing the sagebrush clothing.

The skirt or *Swanake* was not described in the collections Accession notes, but is probably similar to aboriginal sagebrush bark skirts and aprons. Native sagebrush skirts likely were wrap skirts where this is not and certainly would not have had a denim waistband as this one has. This skirt also has decorative fringe flaps topped with small patches of fur, that probably were not present on aboriginal bark skirts intended for daily wear.

To make the clothing Mrs. George pulled long strips of bark from sagebrush and softened the

strips by rubbing them between the knuckles of her clenched fists. She usually twine wove the strips together using cordage made from hemp (dogbane).

In contrast to the more modern and dressy skirt on Page 42, the skirt in *Figure 25* is probably typical of the clothing worn by some Great Basin peoples on a daily basis. When worn it apparently was wrapped around the waist and was attached with a cord or belt similar to what is illustrated in this photograph. This skirt is approximately 28 inches long by 48 inches wide and was made from strips of sagebrush bark twine woven together. The main strands hang vertically and are about one inch wide and were not twisted or processed beyond just being stripped from the plant and torn into strips approximately one inch wide. Four rows of narrower strips of bark were used to twine weave the vertical strips together. The twining was started by laying a strip of bark into the fold of a narrow strand of bark. The two parts of the narrow strips were given a single twist to the left (counter clockwise) then another strand was laid in and twined, (*Figure 26*). This was continued with the four rows of twining until the width of the skirt was obtained. The edge that is assumed to be the top of the skirt was finished in

Figure 25. Typical sagebrush skirt. This skirt is in the collections of the Jerry Lee Young Idaho Heritage Museum, Hollister Idaho.

Figure 26. Sagebrush skirt laid out flat to show how it was constructed. This skirt is in the collections of the Jerry Lee Young Idaho Heritage Museum, Hollister Idaho.

43

a different manner. A one inch wide strip of bark was laid across the vertical strips and it was twined to them by wrapping strips of bark around the top band and then under the vertical strips. This was continued for the width of the skirt.

Figure 27. *Traditional sagebrush top or blouse. This blouse is in the collections of the Jerry Lee Young Idaho Heritage Museum, Hollister Idaho.*

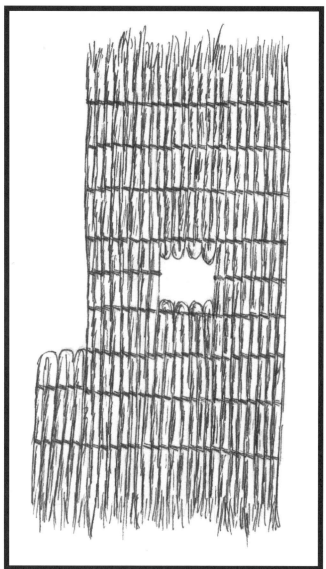

Figure 28. *Sagebrush top laid out flat to show construction.*

The top or blouse (above) is about 28 inches wide and about 29 inches long from the shoulders on the front and about 24 inches long on the back. It has four or five rows of twining both front and back with several rows of twining with cotton string used in making modern repairs.

It was made in a manner similar to, but more complex than the skirt. Approximately one inch wide sagebrush bark strands were twined to-gether with narrow strips of sagebrush bark as described above for the skirt. Several long strands were laid in first that extended from the front over the shoulder and down the back of the garment. Then for the neck hole strands were laid in and folded back on themselves and twined in leaving the neck opening. An extra flap of material was twined on one side which appears to have folded around the side of the body under the arm. There was no matching flap on the other side.

After finding this skirt and top Jerry Young had

a local Indian woman repair them. She used either milkweed or stinging nettle fiber and cotton thread to re-twine portions of the clothing and to stitch them to a burlap backing made from burlap bags. Both the skirt and top are in the collections of Jerry Lee Young's Idaho Heritage Museum, Hollister, Idaho.

BUCKSKIN AND FIBER SKIRTS

CALIFORNIA

The standard dress for California women was a double skirt or apron. Several variations of this arrangement occurred. One style had a fringed buckskin apron in front and a broader apron or skirt in the back that wrapped around to meet the front piece.

Some styles of California women's skirts had a fiber front and a fur skin as the back portion. They were tied on with cords at the waist and had no side seams. The front fibers were apparently draped or tied over the corded belt. A few rows of fibers were twined in horizontally at the top, and below the twining the strands were allowed to hang loose. The fibers had balls of asphalt on the ends supposedly to keep the strands from flying in the wind or possibly for decoration. Other decorations were shells on the sides. The back portion may have been longer than the front which ended several inches above the knee.

A variation to the above California skirt is a buckskin back piece instead of the fur, while the front is fiber. Another variation is both the front and back pieces were sometimes made from skin. The front was narrow with the back piece wider and folding around the hips to meet the front. The bottom half of the front skin was slit into fringe to make walking and sitting easier. Sometimes each strip on the front was wrapped with bear grass or strung with pine nuts.

Fibers used to make these skirts included shred-

ded inner bark of redwood and willow and other trees, tules, milk weed, hemp, and others. Women decorated the ends with bits of tar, tiny shells, pine nuts etc. Some fibers were dyed a bright red.

WRAP SKIRTS

WOMEN, many areas

The term wrap skirt usually refers to a tanned skin or piece of fabric wrapped around the waist. It was held with a belt or tied with cordage or buckskin thongs. Wrap skirts were worn with or without other clothing depending on the climate and weather. In the Plains the wrap skirt was probably one of the earliest forms of clothing. Poncho tops were added as needed and this combination is thought to have evolved into the three skin dress of the Southern Plains.

BUCKSKIN WRAP SKIRTS

Probably the earliest type of buckskin skirt was a natural shaped tanned hide just wrapped around the waist. It may have overlapped on one side slightly depending on the size of the hide. A belt made from corded fibers or a strip of buckskin was then tied around the skirt just below the waist and the top of the hide was rolled down several inches over the belt. This secured the garment. This may be the style described as the Algonquian slit skirt. If the overlap is on the side then a thigh could easily be bared for rolling fibers into cordage as described in the section on the Northeast Woodlands.

To make this skirt simply find a hide of the right size to fit around the persons waist with a little overlap. The length can vary according to desire and availability of hides to choose from. Native skirt lengths varied from very short to ankle length. Then make a fiber cord or cut a strip of buckskin to tie around the hips or waist. Several inches of the hide should be left above

Figure 29. Native way of putting on a wrap skirt.

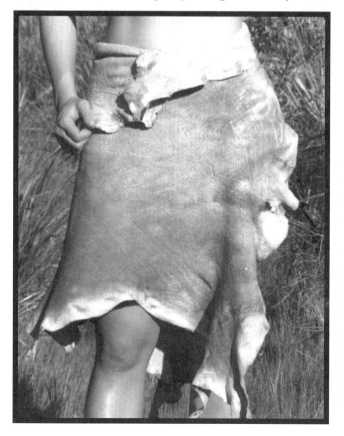

the cord, it is then rolled down over the cord similar to the one in *Figure 29*. For the most primitive or authentic look do not trim the hide but leave it in its natural shape after it is brain tanned. The top folded over portion and the hem will both be uneven. The bottom and edges can be cut into fringe if desired.

Figure 30. Another style of buckskin wrap skirt made by Beata Kubiak. Note how the waist band naturally rolls down. Beata said she does not like fringe but prefers to leave the edges natural.

This wrap skirt is authentic in that it is just buckskin wrapped around the waist and tied on with buckskin thongs. The drawing in *Figure 31* shows the shape of the skirt shown in *Figure 30*. Beata made this skirt from two pieces of hide sewed together. The coyote head top she is wearing is probably not authentic but is a novel idea for someone looking for something unique! To make a wrap skirt similar to this cut a hide or

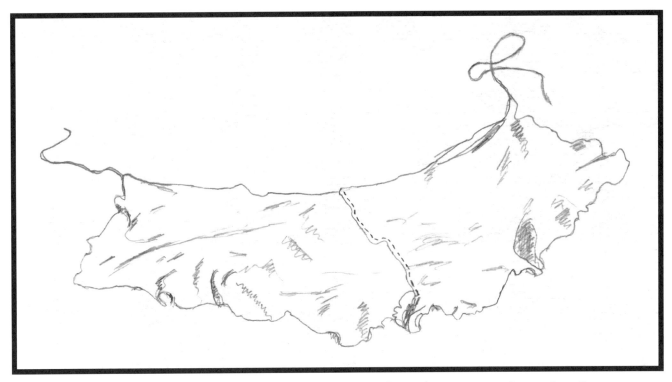

Figure 31. *Beata's wrap skirt laid out flat to show the manner of construction.*

Figure 32

lace pieces of hide together to fit around the waist and overlap as desired. Also cut them to the length desired. Attach a buckskin strap to each side to tie the skirt around the waist. The hem can be cut straight across or it can be left natural for a more primitive look. The hem and edges can be cut into fringe if desired.

BUCKSKIN SKIRTS

Figure 32 is an example of a traditional buckskin skirt. By removing the ties at the side of the skirt it becomes the more primitive buckskin double apron.

This traditional skirt is made from two small hides. The hides were cut even across the top and left somewhat in the natural shape on the sides and bottom. The skins were fringed on the top, bottom and sides. The top was folded down a couple of inches and laced to the skirt to hold the belt as shown in *Figure 33*. The two pieces were laced together at each side in a

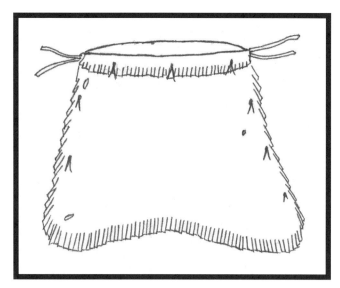

Figure 33. *Drawing showing how the buckskin skirt in* Figure 32 *is made.*

few places. Natives would remove the side ties when wanting more ventilation in hot weather. With the ties removed the skirt becomes a double apron. Women often wore skirts similar to this without other clothing. A poncho top or other simple top was added when weather demanded.

BASKETRY HATS

Figure 34. *Basketry hat worn by Basin peoples.*

BASIN groups were well advanced in making basketry items. Basketry hats were made and

used for a variety of purposes. They developed several types of twining and coiling and used willow and other elements to construct the hats. Women wore basketry hats to protect their heads from burden basket tumplines, they used them as a standard unit of measure for seeds and foods and they doubled as a food bowl. Pictured above is a Paiute Owens Valley close twill basket hat (*Figure 34*).

BREECHCLOUT

A breechclout (also called loincloth or breech-cloth) is a long narrow piece of buckskin or other material that is worn by passing it between the legs and putting it over a belt both in the front and in the back so that flaps hang down in front and back of the persons waist. The length and width of the breechclout varied from area to area. In some cases instead of wearing a belt

Figure 35. *Breechclout and leggings made by Mike Sullivan. Also shown is his daughter wearing a two skin buckskin dress that he made for her.*

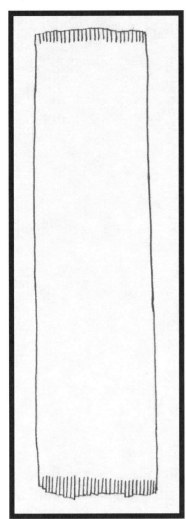

to hold the breechclout, small ties were added to the sides of each flap to tie the breechclout around the waist.

The breechclout seems to be the universal piece of clothing for Indian men in most cultural areas, but it is also reported to have been worn by women in some areas. However it does not appear to have been used by women nearly so much as by men.

Figure 36. Basic breechclout.

MEN, Plains

Osage and Kansas breechclouts were about 12-18 inches wide and they folded or adjusted them for more or less cover according to the weather. It is thought that in some parts of the Plains the normal clothing before traders was a small apron or skin attached to a belt. When the traders came they began wearing breechclouts.

The Northeast Woodlands breechclout was a narrow strip of buckskin about 18 inches wide and three to four feet long. Apparently some wore it either as a breechclout or as a kilt. The long piece of buckskin could be wrapped around the waist to make the kilt or worn between the legs in the traditional breechclout manner.

To make a breechclout cut a piece of buckskin into a rectangle. The width and length varies but can be about 12 to 18 inches wide. To mea-

sure the length run a string or rope between the legs and over the belt both in front and in back. Mark the rope at the desired length and cut the buckskin to that length. Native breechclouts varied in length from just a few inches overlap in front and back to dragging on the ground. Cut fringe in both ends of the breechclout and add beads, quills or other decoration as desired.

CAPOTES

Blanket coats got the name Capote from the early French trappers in the Canadian woods. They were widely used among the fur traders. Indians, frontiersmen and soldiers also adopted the capote and it became popular apparel on the early American frontier. Many capotes were made from Striped Hudson Bay and Whitney blankets. Early blankets had blue or black stripes. Late in the 18th century more colors became available and by the early 19th century candy striped blankets were being produced.

Capotes had many variations in construction, but generally were large with loose fitting sleeves that often had the ends folded into a cuff and they had a belt and pointed hood. A variety of capote patterns are available through outlets that sell leather crafts and mountain man supplies.

Figure 37.

Figure 38.

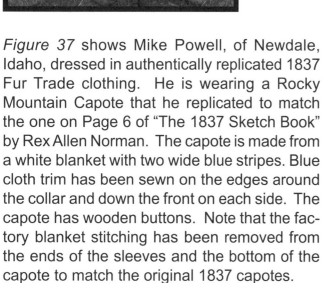

Figure 37 shows Mike Powell, of Newdale, Idaho, dressed in authentically replicated 1837 Fur Trade clothing. He is wearing a Rocky Mountain Capote that he replicated to match the one on Page 6 of "The 1837 Sketch Book" by Rex Allen Norman. The capote is made from a white blanket with two wide blue stripes. Blue cloth trim has been sewn on the edges around the collar and down the front on each side. The capote has wooden buttons. Note that the factory blanket stitching has been removed from the ends of the sleeves and the bottom of the capote to match the original 1837 capotes.

The author made the two capotes, shown in *Figure 38*, using the "Blanket Capote Pattern PM/50" from *Eagles View Patterns*. The light colored capote is made from a used hospital blanket and the other is made from a striped blanket; both blankets are wool. They both have brain tanned buckskin fringe around the neck and on the sleeves. Modeled by Marty and

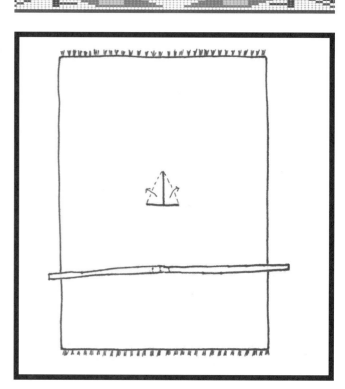

Figure 39. *Design and layout for a simple survival capote.*

50

Dorraine Pool.

Illustrated in *Figure 39* is a practical survival capote that can be made from any blanket and doubles as part of the bedroll at night. Fold a blanket in half and cut a straight slit or a T-slit in the center, as shown in the drawing, for the neck opening. In a survival situation it would then be ready to wear for a capote. A cloth or buckskin strap can be sewed to the back to tie the capote around the waist when worn, or a separate sash or rope could also be used for the same purpose. To keep the neck slit from fraying and to dress it up a little, sew cloth or buckskin edging over the cut edges. If desired put a few holes in the edging and a lace could be used to close the hole, for more warmth, when the capote is being used for a blanket. If desired a simple hood could also be made from scrap material and attached to the capote. When using the survival capote for a blanket flop the hood over the neck hole.

DRESSES

RECTANGLE DRESS

WOMEN, Southwest - Blanket or Rectangle Dress

Woven rectangles of cloth, usually cotton or wool, were made into dresses that were wrapped around the body and attached over the right shoulder and under the left arm leaving the left shoulder bare. A narrow sash of many colors was tied around the body to hold the dress. They were often decorated with colors and geometric designs. Pueblo women dyed their dresses blue with extracts from sunflower seeds.

Early rectangle dresses were either two blankets tied together over one shoulder or just one blanket wrapped around the body and tied over the shoulder as above. Each were held in place with a sash tied around the waist.

Figure 40. Southwest blanket dress.

The dress shown in *Figure 40* demonstrates what an early Southwest style dress may have looked like. The author purchased some coarse woven natural cotton to make the dress. The cloth was dyed light brown by soaking it in water and black walnut husks.

The pattern is simple. The cloth is cut just long enough to go from the woman's shoulder to about the knee and wide enough to fit loosely around her body. A couple of stitches were put in the top right corner to hold the dress over her right shoulder. This dress is worn over the right shoulder and under the left shoulder. The side seam was sewed from the hem up to above the waist to provided a large loose arm hole. The bottom was cut into a fringe and when washed it formed a ragged edge. Created next is a long sash about three inches wide and long enough to be used as a belt.

In old drawings and photos an alternate method, used by the Navaho, of wearing the dress is illustrated in *Figure 41*. It appears that two blankets are used instead of one. The blankets are attached together over both shoulders and a wide neckline is formed, sometimes falling off one or both shoulders. The blankets are probably sewed or tied together on the sides and a belt is shown wrapped around the waist. The blankets appear to be sewed or tied from the sides of the neck opening out to the edge forming the sleeves.

HALTER TOP DRESS

Figure 42 is drawing of a halter top dress made by the Havasupai. This is a two skin dress with a neck strap to hold the front part up, The back part ties at the waist leaving the back bare from the waist up. Sometimes the breast flap was decorated. Fringe was cut along the bottom and sides.

Making a halter top dress.
To make the front of the dress fold the neck of the hide down to form a flap or yoke and attach a neck strap as shown in the illustration. The dress should extend from above the bust to the ankle or to the desired length. The back portion of the dress is made by cutting a hide that would go from the waist to the length of the front hide. The back piece is tied to the front piece at the waist and a buckskin belt is worn over the dress. Fringe and other decorations can be added as desired.

Figure 41. Some of the Navaho wore a blanket dress that attached over both shoulders. Drawing by Cheryl Vierstra

STRAP DRESS

WOMEN, Plains and many other areas
Strap Dress or Slip and Sleeve Dress

A dress of skin with shoulder straps was made similar to a woman's modern slip. The length varied from above the knee to ankle length. In addition to the shoulder straps it had separate sleeves that could be added in cold weather. From the sleeves came the name "slip and sleeve dress". The sleeves were attached behind the back and sometimes tied under the arms or in front of the chest. The dress could be decorated with fringe, quills and deer and elk teeth.

The strap dress seems to have been worn over a longer period of time and a wider geographic area than the similar side seam dress.

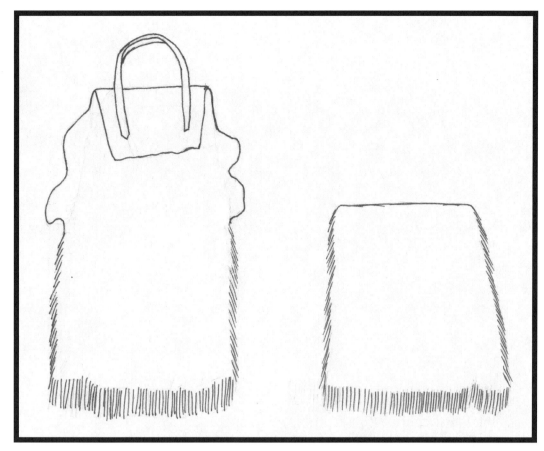

Figure 42. The Havasupai made a dress with a halter top.

Figure 43. Basic strap dress showing one style of sleeves.

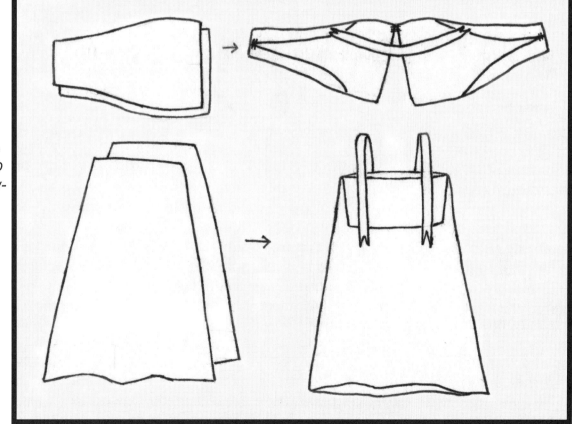

An older version of the strap dress was a short blouse with shoulder straps that was worn in combination with a wrap skirt.

A basic strap (or slip and sleeve) dress can be made using *Figure 43* and the following instructions:

Trim two hides to the basic pattern as shown in the drawings. The top portion is folded down to form a small flap in the front and back. Sew, lace or tie the sides together as shown and add shoulder straps. Or if a large enough skin is available it can be folded in half, sewed together on the side and the top portion folded down as described.

Several different types of sleeves were made by the Indians depending on locale, but a basic sleeve can be made using the accompanying drawing as a guide. The sleeves are attached together in the back and a strap is added to hold the sleeves across the front of the neck or chest. The sleeves are left open underneath but are attached at the wrist. An alternate method of attaching the sleeves is to attach two thongs or strings, as shown in *Figure 5* and tie them together, one set in front of the neck and the other set in back of the neck.

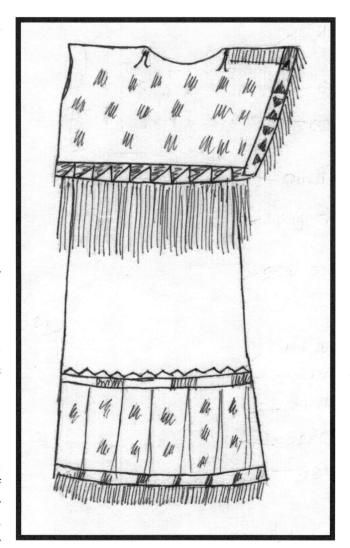

Figure 44. *Plains Cree style side fold dress.*

SIDE FOLD DRESS

WOMEN, Plains
It appears that on the northern Plains the side fold dress was transitional between the strap dress and the two skin dress. A side fold dress is considered a one skin dress but was made from two skins joined together if needed. An elk or large deer hide was folded in half along the backbone and then the top was folded down similar to the strap dress. The open side was laced up leaving an opening at the top for the arm, then the other arm hole was cut in the top of the folded side. To finish it the top was laced or tied together leaving a neck opening.

Figure 44 is a Plains Cree style dressy side fold dress. This dress is decorated with fringe, quill wrapped fringe at the shoulders and quill wrapped thongs hanging from the skirt. Turquoise and white bead bands are on the shoulder and across the lower part of the skirt. The yoke and skirt have bands of quillwork and blotches of orange ochre painted on them.

Making a Side Fold Dress
Fold the hide as shown in *Figure 45* or if needed piece a couple of hides together then fold. Fold the top down to form a yoke and the sleeves. Cut an arm hole on the folded side. Sew or lace the hide together on top of the shoulders leaving an opening for the neck. Sew or lace

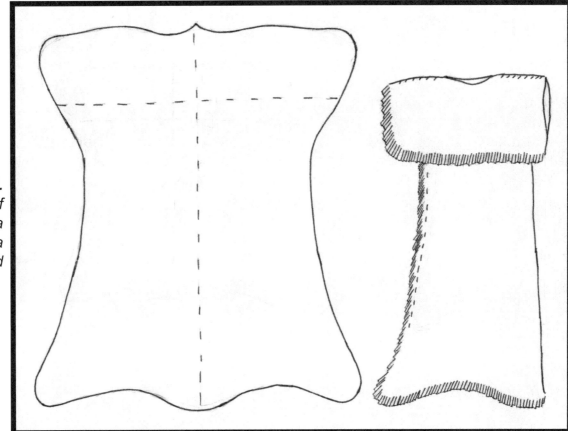

Figure 45. *Method of folding a hide for a side fold dress.*

the side of the dress together from below the sleeve down as shown. Cut fringe and add decorations as desired.

Decorations: Early Plains side fold dresses were decorated with paint or small areas of quill work. Teeth and shells were also used. Scored or incised lines on the buckskin were used and when available brass beads and pony beads were used.

TWO SKIN DRESS

T Shaped, or Two Skin, Dresses were made by either tying or sewing two skins together on the shoulders and down the sides, with apparently no tailoring. Materials used were usually deer but also elk, mountain sheep and antelope were used. The dress usually had a belt. They are sometimes called a binary dress or deer tail dress because the animals tails were usually

Figure 46. *Hidatsa two skin dress with simulated elk teeth decorations.*

left on in center front and back.

Figure 46 is a two skin dress, probably Hidatsa or Mandan, from about 1900 to 1915. It appears that the front and back half of the dress were made by cutting the hides, and possibly piecing sections in to form the identical front and back T-shaped halves of the dress. The two halves were sewed together along the top of the shoulders and down the sides. The buckskin was made from elk or deer. It has eight circular rows of simulated elk teeth, with a partial ninth row around the neck opening. The teeth are made from both bone and antler and some have a dark brown stain applied to them to imitate the caries on teeth from older animals. This dress has short fringe on the sleeves and in the side seams and a longer fringe on the bottom. Some fringe on the bottom is cut into the dress but there are also panels of fringe that were sewed to the bottom. The bottom of the sleeves are open from the armpit. The neck opening was made by cutting a cross opening and each corner was then folded over and sewed down forming a diamond shaped neck opening. This dress is part of the Rev. Harold Case collection, Fort Berthold, Theodore Roosevelt Medora Foundation, Museum of the Badlands collection.

WOMEN, Northern Plains
A basic two skin dress consisted of two skins, usually deer or elk sewed together, one for the front and one for the back. The hind quarters of the hides were folded down, one over the chest and one over the back, to form the yoke and sleeves. A small strip of hair and the tail was often left on the edge forming a decorative hair fringe at the bottom of the yoke. The dress was sewed up the sides to the waist or bust and had a wide belt that was fastened in the back.

Quills, beads, elk ivory and fringe were added above the hair fringe of the yoke for additional decoration. The seams and bottom of the dress were fringed and decorated with elk teeth and beads according to tribal customs; elk teeth being valued above other forms of ornamentation. Catlin's drawings show several dresses with circles of beads or quills on the breast and with short cords of beads hanging from the center of the circle.

WOMEN, Plateau, Coeur d'Alene
Plateau women made two skin dresses similar to the Plains style described above with the front and back hindquarters folded over to form the yokes. A third skin was used to lengthen the hem and even it up or to add fullness to the skirt if needed. The sleeves were usually left open underneath, the sides and bottoms of the sleeves were always fringed. Beads, pendants, tassels, etc. were added for decoration.

Figure 47. *Two skin dress. Note the yoke folded down with hair fringe and tail in front.*

GIRLS, Basin

Dresses were made from two fawn skins with the hair left on the outside. The dresses were made similar to a woman's two skin dress except that there was no folded over yoke in the front and back. Buckskin fringe and thongs were added to the front and back.

Making a two skin dress

To make a two skin dress try to pick two skins about the same size. When scraping the hair off the hides leave the tail intact and a one inch strip of hair along the rump of the skin. Tan and break the hides. It may be difficult to get the hide soft along the edge where the hair strip is left on, but work it as soft as possible. As shown in *Figure 48*, the rear hair strip and tail of the hides will become the front and back yokes and sleeves of the dress when completed. The yokes will hang down with the hair side out.

Leave the neck and forelegs of the deerskin in their natural shape as much as possible to form an uneven hemline. (Note, if a person does not want to tan the hides with the hair strip on or is using hides already tanned without the hair strip, a suitable, though not authentic, substitute would be to trim the hides to the proper shape and sew strips of fur to the edges.)

Lay the two hides down flat and sew or lace them together in a straight line a few inches below the rump and tail as shown in *Figure 48*. Leave a neck opening. Punch holes with an awl and stitch in a running stitch with narrow buckskin thongs or heavy thread. Fold the tail sections down in front and back and lace them to the dress in the same manner. The stitches should be just above the hair strip on the edge of the skin. The sides are sewed together also using a running stitch a short distance in from

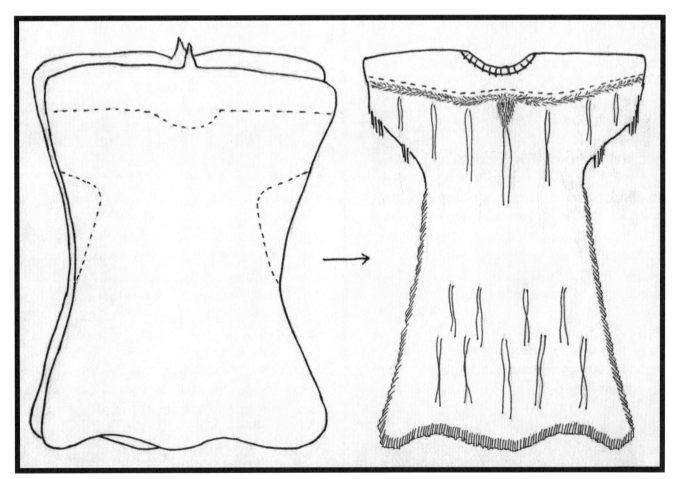

Figure 48. *Basic pattern for a two skin dress.*

the edges of the skin. Excess skin is cut into fringe. For a more primitive look the sides can be just tied together in a few places with buckskin thongs.

If desired, before sewing the sides, trim a small amount of the hide from the two sides under the arms to shape the hide as shown in the drawings. Early dresses were made from hides left in the natural shape and were more flowing because of the fringe; later, clothing was more tailored and made from hides that were trimmed to shape and were probably a little less flowing. When making the dress make it a few inches larger than the bust and hip measurements, since the dress is intended to be quite loose fitting. The side seams are sewn from the bottom up to the waist or the bust line. Nursing Indian mothers would sew the side seams up to just the waist. To add more fullness to the bottom of the dress and to allow more freedom of movement triangular gussets can be sewed in the side seams. More freedom of movement can also be accomplished by starting the side seams above the knee and going up. The sleeves formed by the yoke are not sewed shut along the bottom.

Authentic dresses commonly had pieces of buckskin added to the bottom of the dress to lengthen it, to emphasize the pattern formed by the neck and legs, to make the hem line even, and/or to add fringe. When making a two skin dress, if the hides are not properly shaped, lace pieces in where needed to fill out and shape the dress and it will still be authentically made.

Yokes
Two skin dresses had several variations of yoke attachments which are illustrated in *Figure 49* and described below:

Fig. 49 (a) When the skins are a little short, the rump and tail portion can be cut off in a straight line. The two pieces of skin cut from the rump can be sewn together to make a yoke which is

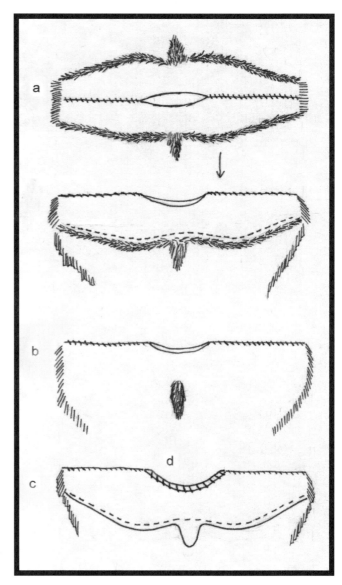

Figure 49. *Two skin dress yoke variations.*

then sewed to the skins as shown above. As can be seen by the drawing, this adds a few inches to the length of the dress. If the portions cut from the rump are not sufficient for a yoke then a separate yoke can be made from other pieces of hide and sewed to the skins.

(b) Though not as common as the above methods, the skins were sometimes cut straight across the rump and sewed together without adding the yoke. Sometimes the tail was sewed on under the neckline.

(c) The yoke could be made without the hair

strip on the edge. The deer tail skin could be left on or a piece of skin was sewed on that was cut to the shape of the tail.

(d) Red trade cloth was sometimes laced into the neck opening of the dress with a buckskin thong.

Decorations

There are many variations of native decorations for two skin dresses reported. Often the only decoration was abundant fringe and the deer tails hanging in the front and back of the dress yoke. Fringe was usually cut into the edges of the skin along the sides and bottom of the skirt and also along the bottom of the sleeves. Or pieces of buckskin could be inserted into the seams and cut into fringe. In addition long fringe was attached to the yoke and the skirt in various patterns. *Figure 50* shows several ways of attaching long fringe strips to the body of the dress.

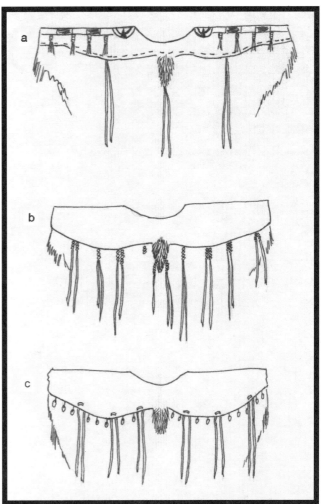

Figure 51. Two skin dress yoke decorations.

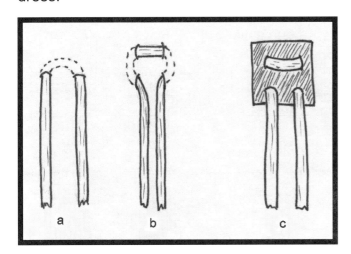

Figure 50. Methods of attaching buckskin thongs to a dress. (a) loop the thong through two holes, (b) loop it through four holes, (c) Attach a piece of red trade cloth or felt by looping the thong through matching holes.

Figure 48 shows a plain dress with minimal decorations. It has the hair strip on the yoke; long fringe is attached to the yoke along the hair strip and to the skirt of the dress; All the free edges are cut into fringe and a piece of red trade

cloth is laced to the neckline with buckskin thongs.

Yoke decorations

The yokes of the two skin dresses were beaded or quilled in a number of different ways. Bands of beads or quills were put along the top of the shoulders and around the neck opening. They were sometimes put just above the hair strip on the yoke or just under the hair strip of the yoke.

In *Figure 51*, the first drawing (a) shows bands of beads or quills on the shoulder seam with rosettes on both sides near the neck opening. It also has horse hair strips wrapped with quills. The next drawing (b) shows a plain yoke with no hair strip and has beads hanging on thongs that dangle from the yoke. The third drawing (c) shows elk teeth and cowry shells attached to the plain yoke.

Another form of decorating two skin dresses was hanging thongs from the yoke in various places with beads attached.

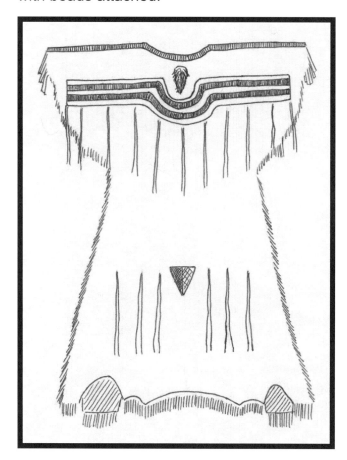

Figure 52. *Blackfoot dress with typical decoration.*

Figure 52 above is a Blackfoot dress with similar decoration: Bands of beadwork are on the top of the shoulder and around the neck opening; the tail is sewed below the neckline; bands of beads are on the front of the yoke (breastband) and follow the contour around the tail. Long fringe hangs from the beadwork and is also attached on the skirt while red trade cloth patches are sewed to the hem of the dress; a red and blue trade cloth triangle is attached to the center of the front of the dress. The Blackfoot triangular or heart shaped patches are

thought to be a sign of womanhood, the center triangle represents the woman's uterus and the bottom patches her ovaries. Some references however indicate that the triangular patch is an effigy of the animals head.

The Blackfoot dress, in *Figure 52*, does not have a folded down or sewed on yoke. A variation to this style was to fold down a large yoke leaving the hair and tail attached. Bands of quills or beads were put on the yoke and dipped down in the center just above the tail. Bands of beads or quills were also put on the shoulder seams and around the neckline.

The Blackfoot breastband was usually made from several solid bands of two contrasting light and dark colors, black and white being the most common. Light blue and black, dark blue and white, and pink and green are all reported. Even when the dresses did not have the tails, or later when they were made from cloth the breastbands of beads were sewed in a contour as though it were going around the tail.

Crow two skin dresses were decorated with quills similar to Blackfoot dresses except that the breastband did not always dip in the center under the tail. They were usually decorated with many elk teeth.

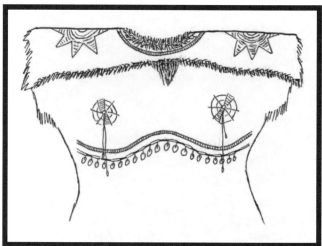

Figure 53. *Mandan yoke and decorations from a drawing by George Catlin.*

60

A Mandan dress is shown in *Figure 53.*. A drawing done by Geroge Catlin of a Mandan woman shows a dress with decorations similar to this illustration. It has the hair strip and tail attached; the neckline has a band of beading or quills around it; there is a beaded or quilled rosette centered on each side of the bustline, from the center of each rosette a few beads hang from buckskin thongs; there is a narrow strip of beads below the bust with a number of elk teeth or cowry shells hanging from it and finally there is a large quilled or beaded eight point star on each shoulder. Mandans used blue and green beadwork and quilled rosettes of yellow, blue and red.

Assiniboines are reported to have used black and white or light blue and white for their bead or quill work. Paiutes preferred to use black, red, blue and white. The Snake, however, used light blue and white beadwork.

THREE SKIN DRESS

WOMEN, Plains

Early southern Plains women made a three skin dress by cutting two skins across just below the forelegs and then sewing, lacing or tying the sides together. Early skirts were just attached together in a few places with buckskin thongs along the sides. These ties could be loosened or removed in warm weather for more ventilation. A third skin was folded along the back bone, a neck slit was cut in the fold and the top was sewed or tied to the skirt in front and back at the waist. The sides of the top were left open and the sleeves were not sewed underneath. Fringe was cut into the edges of the hides.

A Sioux three piece buckskin dress from about 1920-1930 is shown in *Figure 54*. It has scattered simulated elk teeth, made from bone, sewn onto the dress. There are thongs with beads attached on the lower portion of the dress. The dress was pieced together from several smaller pieces of skin, and additional pieces of buckskin were added to the original dress to lengthen the sleeves. There is long fringe on the sleeves, yoke and bottom of the skirt. The yoke is hair side out and appears to be wet-scraped when tanned, while the skirt has some pieces flesh side out and some pieces hair side out. This fine dress is part of the collection of the Standing Rock Sioux, Theodore Roosevelt Medora Foundation, Museum of the Badlands.

WOMEN, Plateau

A three skin dress (plains influenced) was made by Plateau women using two skins for the skirt and a third for the top. A hole was cut in the middle of the top skin for the neck opening and strings or thongs were attached at the sides of the neck for closures.

A common winter three skin dress was made similarly, only the hair was left on the top skin.

Figure 54. Sioux three skin dress.

61

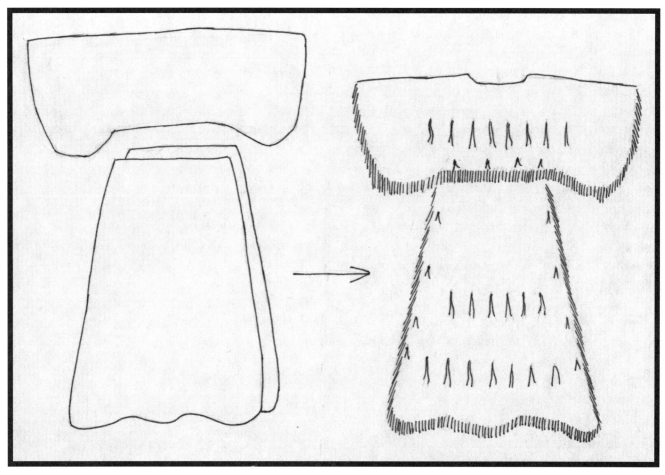

Figure 55. *This is a basic three skin dress with fringe being the only decoration. This would be considered an everyday garment. In making a plain dress like this the hides should be left in their natural shape as much as possible and the pieces tied or laced together with buckskin thongs for a more primitive look.*

Sometimes the hair was also left on the bottom skins. The skins used were from yearling does.

Making a Three Skin Dress

As shown in *Figure 55*, to make a three skin dress pick two similar sized skins for the skirt and a third skin for the top or yoke. Trim the two skirt skins to the general shape shown in the drawing. Trim just below the forelegs or just trim the ends of the forelegs off. Some sources indicate that the skirt was made with the neck and forelegs down as in the two skin dress. If using this method just trim the rear legs off and trim the skirt to shape. Since the rear portion of a hide is usually wider than the front it seems to make more sense to use the front of the skin for

the top of the skirt not the bottom. The two skirt pieces are then sewn, laced or tied together along the sides. Ties should be attached a short distance in from the edge so that the edge of the skin can be cut into fringe. Also the bottom can be fringed.

The top skin is folded along the backbone and a slit is cut for the neck hole. As was sometimes done in authentic dress, a cut can be made in the front of the neck hole and ties attached to close the opening after the dress is pulled on over the head. This top is then attached to the skirt by one of the methods described above. The sleeves are left open underneath. All free edges are cut into fringe. The top skin can be left in its natural shape, trimmed to a symmetrical shape or false legs can be attached to give it a more natural shape.

Figure 56. Three skin buckskin dress made by the author.

The dress shown above was made similarly to the three skin dress described above. For the skirt part two skins were trimmed straight across the top but were otherwise left in the same shape they were when tanned. For the top of the dress, a neck slit was cut in the center of another skin as shown. Two small slits about 1/4 inch apart were cut, then small buckskin strips were used to tie the pieces together. First the two bottom pieces were attached to the top then the side ties were added to hold the dress together. Six or seven ties were used on both the front and back to hold the top to the skirt and three were added down each side. Though not necessarily authentic, two pieces of hide were added at

the neck line and cut into fringe. The sleeves were not attached under the arms and all edges were cut into fringe.

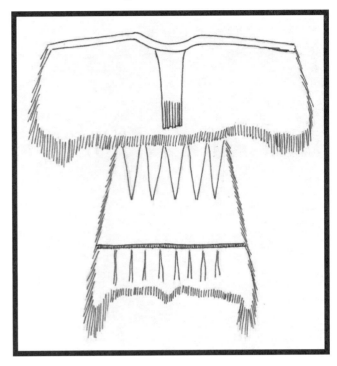

Figure 57. Comanche three skin dress.

The author's conception of a Comanche three skin dress described by Wallace and Hoebel is illustrated in *Figure 57*. The skirt was made with two skins with the legs still attached on the bottom making an uneven hemline to the ankles. The sides of the two skins were sewed together with buckskin thongs. Heavy fringe was cut in the skin from the bottom up to just above the knees, from there lighter fringe extended up the side of the skirt. The top was made from a third skin that had a slit cut in it for the neck opening and was attached to the skirt with buckskin laces. The top skin formed large wide sleeves that were heavily fringed. Attached to the top was a *peplum*, or piece of hide cut into long points that hung down to about mid-thigh. An additional strip of buckskin was hung down from the neck in the front and back on dresses of the number one wives of brave warriors. On this flap of buckskin, symbols for each war honor and *coup* her husband achieved was painted.

The skirt was decorated with a band of beads above the knee line with long buckskin thongs hanging below the beads. The top was decorated with geometric designs and colored beads scattered along by the fringe.

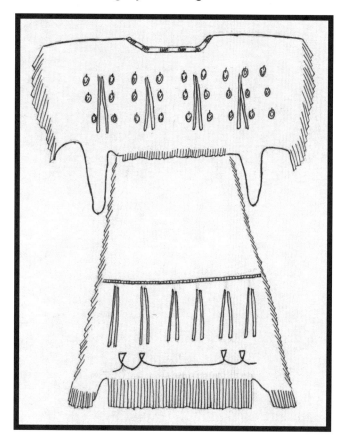

Figure 58. *Kiowa three skin dress.*

In addition to fringe the Kiowa dress shown in *Figure 58* has beadwork on the neck with elk teeth or cowry shells attached to the yoke. The skirt has a row of red beads around the center and buckskin thongs hanging from the row. The bottom of the skirt also has a band of dark blue, light blue and white beads. Each piece of fringe on the bottom is attached separately.

Variations of three skin dresses

The three skin dress is thought to have originated from a skirt and separate poncho top. The poncho top was just a hide with a neck hole in the center that was put on over the head and worn without being attached to the skirt. This variation is a transitional form between a skirt and a dress. If desiring to portray this variation a woman would wear the top unattached to the skirt.

Fringe on the clothing is optional and could be left off for one extreme. The other extreme would be to add pieces of buckskin to the dress to cut into additional fringe.

The top hide can be cut to a uniform symmetrical shape or it can be left in the natural shape with the legs hanging down on the sides; long fringe can be cut into the legs if desired. Also pieces can be added to simulate legs.

The neck slit can be cut straight across the top and if desired an additional vertical slit can be cut in the front and ties added to close it after putting the dress on over the head.

Some old dresses had a longer neck slit with a tie or two on the sides of the neck to lace the opening shut with after putting the dress on.

The skirt bottom could be cut into a number of different patterns and fringed in several ways. The Kiowa laced in each piece of fringe separately through a hole punched in the bottom of the skirt.

Decorations

There was great variation in the type of decoration for the three skin dress. The following are some examples that were used in traditional times.

Top or Yoke
The yoke was left plain or fringe was cut into the edges in various patterns. The Kiowa and others often dyed the yoke yellow with buffalo gallstones. Elk teeth, cowry shells and other items were attached directly to the yoke or hung from thongs. The neck opening was left plain or bound with colored trade cloth or was banded

with beads. The legs were sometimes left on the yoke or false legs were attached. Dew claws were sometimes left on the legs or reattached. Breastbands of quills or beads were placed on the yoke following the contour as though the tail were attached.

Skirt

The skirt was usually at least fringed on the edges and bottom and could also have long fringe attached to it in one or several rows. The bottom of the skirt was cut to one of various shapes. Bands of beads were attached across the center and along the bottom. Paint was also used at times for the designs across the bottom. For example:

Dakota Sioux - Red and blue on a white background for neck and shoulder bands. Red and white band on center and bottom of skirt.

Oglala Sioux - Breastband of green and red, neck and shoulder bands of light and dark blue on a green background.

Arapaho - Used pigment on the skins with small amounts of quill or beadwork. Elk teeth and cowrie shells were also used.

Kiowa and Comanche - Usually large areas of yellow or green pigment. Narrow band of beadwork around the neck line, midpoint of skirt, and hemline. The neck band beads were usually blue and red on a white background and the row of beads across the skirt was red.

Cheyenne - Typical decoration was a band of beads on the front and back of the yoke and a band across the shoulders. These bands were box or border designs. Older dresses had zig zag lines of beadwork around the hemline with the area between the beads and hemline painted red or yellow. Elk teeth and shells were also used. The neck band was of blue and white.

Ute - Rows of blue and white seed beads along

the bottom of the yoke.

Examples of three skin dresses

Figure 59. *Three skin dress from North Dakota.*

Figure 59 illustrates a three skin buckskin dress, probably Hidatsa, from about 1910-1925. It has a fully beaded yoke with a white background, American Flag with four point design, four winds or a star. The beads are red, yellow, blue and green on top. It has an "hour glass" design which might indicate the front and rear sides of a tipi or possibly the "positive-negative" aspect referred to by some. The two bottom beaded bands and the inverted "V" shape band have red and white beads. The skirt portion has fringe with cowrie shells hanging from them. There are leg tabs (not evident in the photograph) at the sides of the bottom edge. This buckskin dress appears to be flesh side out and is about 34 inches across the top of the sleeves and

65

about 50 inches long. This dress may be seen in the Rev. Harold Case collection, Fort Berthold, Theodore Roosevelt Medora Foundation, Museum of the Badlands collection.

across the sleeves on top and 50 inches long. This dress is from the Rev. Harold Case collection, Fort Berthold, Theodore Roosevelt Medora Foundation, Museum of the Badlands collection.

Figure 60. *Three skin dress, note the "U" shape beading which represents where the tail would be on a more traditonal two skin dress.*

Figure 61. *Typical Sioux three skin dress.*

Shown above in *Figure 60* is a three skin buckskin dress with "leg tabs" at the sides of the bottom edge, from about 1910-1930. The designs are the same front and back. Probably Hidatsa with Sioux influence as noted by the "U" shape beading on the center of the front. The fully beaded yoke has a yellow background with red, white, blue and green beaded designs. The breastband and shoulder bands are made with red, blue, and white beads. In addition to the sleeve, side and bottom fringe there are three rows of fringes tied on the body of the dress. The top portion of the dress is hair side out with the skirt being flesh side out. The seams are whipped stitched. It is about 47 inches

Shown above is an Oglala Sioux woman's three skin buckskin dress. This dress was made for Ralph Hubbard by Emma Stirk, an Oglala Sioux Indian woman, in Manderson, South Dakota in the early 1970's. The design is very typically Sioux. As was often the case, she ran out of blue beads for the background and when she purchased more to complete her work the colors did not match perfectly because they were from a different "dye lot."

In addition to the blue bead background there are white beads on the yoke and a row of red beads along the bottom of the yoke. The patterns on the shoulders include white, yellow and red beads. The neck has a red edge made from felt. There is a row of blue beads on the bottom of the dress, and blue and red beads on the front of the dress with thongs hanging down from them. Emma was nearly 90 years old when she made this dress and in spite of her age she did much of this work without the aid of spectacles. She was present during the time of the Wounded Knee Massacre in 1890. Used by permission of the Native American Collection, Gordon B. Olson Library, Minot State University, Minot, North Dakota. Photographed by Joseph C. Jastrzembski.

KILT

MEN, Eastern Forest

A kilt is a straight piece of buckskin wrapped around the waist and overlapped similar to a wrap skirt. A thong was wrapped around below the waist and the top of the skin was rolled down over the thong. This same piece of buckskin could be used as a breechclout as well. For a woman a kilt would be a wrap skirt.

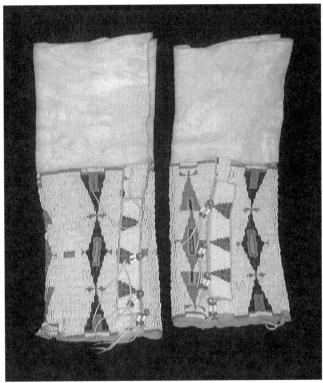

Figure 62. Woman's beaded buckskin leggings.

LEGGINGS

Leggings were common wear for many groups and basically were pieces of skin or other material made similar to a pant leg and worn over the legs. They were worn for warmth and to protect the legs from scratches when traveling through brush. Men's leggings usually came up to the hip and were held up by strips of buckskin over the belt. Some Northeast Woodland men wore knee or thigh length leggings, but mostly to the hip also. Women's leggings usually came to about the knee but sometimes they wore leggings to the hip.

Leggings were made in the Basin by just wrapping hide or sagebrush bark around the legs. Tules were twine woven into leggings by the California. Comanche leggings were tight fitting, extending to the hip and often had a wide margin and long fringe. Leggings with wide

margins and long fringe are thought to be the origin of cowboy chaps.

In the Plains the oldest style of men's leggings was made from hides left pretty much in their natural shape. The hind quarter of the hide was at the top and went around the thigh and the front of the skin went around the ankle. The sides of the skin were tied or laced together and the leggings were held up with buckskin thongs or the hind legs tied to the belt.

Women's Plains leggings were made from pieces of skin cut into trapezoidal or rectangular pieces. They usually went from the top of the moccasin to just below the knee. They were held up with a garter or tie strap. Sometimes the leggings extended to above the knee. These were attached at the top with a strap or garter and excess was folded down over the tie.

Leggings were decorated with fringe, paint,

quills, beads and other forms of decorations.

A good example of this may be seen in *Figure 62* which shows fully beaded women's buckskin leggings from the Sioux. Part of the mirror imaging is shown in this design with the inverted tipi and smoke flap pattern in both blue and green. The red squares could show respect for the ant colonies. These may be seen in the Native American Collection, Gordon B. Olson Library, Minot State University, Minot, North Dakota. They were photographed by Joseph C. Jastrzembski.

Figure 63. *Mans leggings, with fringe as the only decoration.*

Shown above (*Figure 63*) are men's leggings from moose or elk buckskin, Chippewa or Metis, from about 1925-1935. They are Plain leggings with fringe attached to the side seams. The

hides appear to be well smoked and the leggings are made with the flesh side out. They are about 28 inches long. These fine leggings are part of the Jack Stewart collection originally from Turtle Mountain North Dakota.

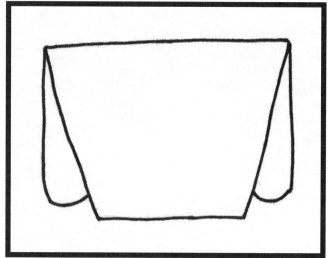

Figure 64. *Pattern for basic women's leggings.*

Making Women's Plains Style Leggings
These leggings are basically tubes of skin worn around the legs. They should go from the ankle to the knee and fit fairly snug. They can be made from buckskin approximately 15" x 12" x 22" as shown in *Figure 64*. Measure around the ankle and calf and add a little for seam allowances and for ease of putting them on and off. Cut buckskin according to the adjusted pattern. Flaps can be added into the seam and fringe cut into the buckskin and other decorations added as desired. This basic pattern can be modified or other patterns made to replicate specific types of women's leggings.

Making Men's Leggings
To make men's leggings, obtain two deer hides that are matched for size and are the right length to cover the leg from about the hip to the ankles. Cut the leggings from the skin using the pattern in the drawing as a guide. (*Figure 65*). The seams are tied, laced or sewed together. Measure first to be sure the leggings will fit around the leg before cutting. Attach a strip of buck-

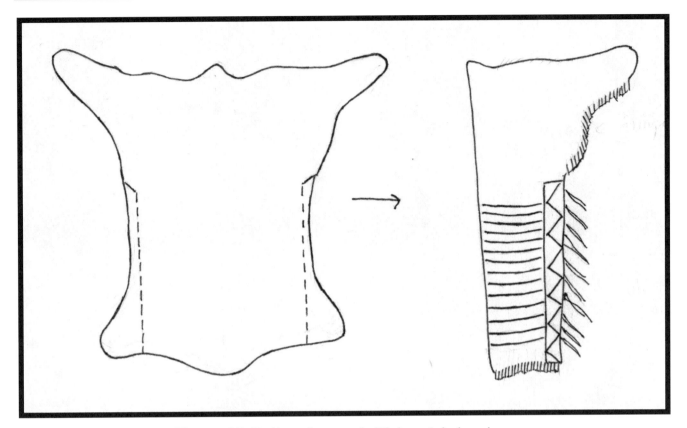

Figure 65. *Pattern for men's Plains style leggings.*

skin to the outside top of the leggings to tie them to the belt.

Common decorations were painted horizontal lines, fringe, beaded strips, beads, deer hooves, and/or hair and fur attached to the beaded strips.

MOCCASINS

Moccasins, the universal footwear of the Native Americans, were as varied as the people themselves. A description of the many types will not be attempted here as each group developed their own particular style of moccasins. An excellent resource for more details on moccasins types and how to make over two dozen different kinds is a booklet titled *Craft Manual of the North American Indian Footwear* by George M. White. His descriptions cover making simple center seam styles to much more advanced style moccasins. There are also other good

references in the literature on making moccasins.

PLAINS

For winter, boots or moccasins were made from buffalo hides with the hair inside. The Plains people developed right and left foot moccasins during a time when white men were still wearing shoes that were the same for each foot. The Plains Indians originally used a soft sole moccasin but when they started spreading to the South and West they added a hard sole to protect their feet from the rocks and cacti of the area. The addition of the hard sole also coincided with the introduction of the steel awl into the Plains Tribes since a steel awl was needed to pierce the heavy sole material. This coincidence may be why it is thought that hard sole moccasins were white inspired.

Basic work moccasins from deerskin with rawhide soles and no decoration are shown in *Fig-*

69

Figure 66. Basic work moccasins.

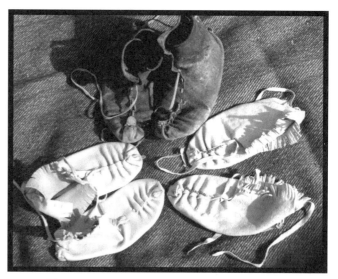

Figure 67. Center seam moccasins

ure 66. They are from the Standing Rock Sioux, from around 1915-1925. They have a "welted seam" around the sole and show signs of use but also long storage. They are from the Jack Stewart collection.

Center seam moccasins are shown in *Figure 67*, above and to the right. The two bottom pair have fringe cut in the tops that are folded down when wearing. The other pair is a higher top style, worn with the tops up and wrapped around the ankle.

Making Center Seam Moccasins
The following are simple instructions for making center seam moccasins:

1. Take measurements as

shown on the drawing using a string.

2. Draw a moccasin pattern as shown below using these measurements; allow a little extra room for lacing holes. The pattern can be adjusted if a higher top moccasin is desired.

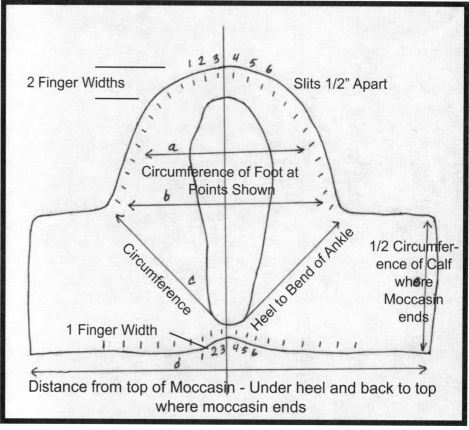

Figure 68. Pattern for center seam moccasins.

3. Cut out two moccasins. Cut lacing slits about 1/8 inch long or punch small holes.

4. Cut two 1/8 inch wide laces about a foot long for each moccasin. Tie the end of each lace to hole # 3 or 4 on the toe and heel.

5. Lace a short piece of strong string in a running stitch through holes 1-6, pull into a pucker and tie.

6. Lace the moccasin together using running stitches with leather thongs through the remaining holes.

7. An optional way to lace the moccasins together is to tie the lace to hole #1 and lace in a running stitch through holes 1 - 6, pull it into a pucker then lace the moccasin together using a running stitch through the remaining holes.

8. Insoles or heavier buckskin soles may be added if desired.

9. The moccasins can be decorated with beads, quills, fringe or other materials as desired.

10. When wearing the moccasin tie the front and back laces together. The tops can be folded and laced down or they can be left up for a higher top style

PARKA

MEN and WOMEN, Arctic and Subarctic
A parka is the upper clothing made like a pullover coat that was worn in the severe winters of the North. They had both inner parkas with the hair towards the body and outer parkas with the hair to the outside. Inner and outer pants were worn with the parkas. Men's parkas had tails that ended at about the hips. Women's parkas generally had long tails, the back one longer than the front one. They had large hoods, a pouch like back where they put their babies and wide armholes so that the mother could bring her baby around to the front inside to nurse.

Parkas varied from area to area but followed the same basic design. It took at least three skins for the parka, one for the front, one for the back and one for the sleeves. They were made from caribou and other furs and were sometimes elaborately decorated. Decorations included fringe, beads, teeth, metal, cloth, dyed bands of skin and other ornaments.

PONCHO TOP

WOMEN, Plains
Wichita women wore a short poncho made by cutting a hole in the center of a single deerskin. It was worn over a skirt in cool weather.

Comanche women made a poncho top (blouse) by cutting a horizontal slit in the center of a skin; this made a high straight neckline. The sleeves were wide and butterfly like and not sewn underneath. The blouse and skirt were laced together at the waist with buckskin thongs. (Technically this would be a three skin dress). Bands of beads were applied that went from elbow to elbow on the sleeves. Beads were also sewed scattered above the fringe on the sleeves.

Making a Poncho Top

A basic primitive poncho top can be made by simply cutting a slit in a deer hide as shown in *Figure 69*, on the next page; depending on the size and shape of the hide the slit could be cut either from side to side or front to back as shown. The skin is then slipped over the head and worn like a poncho. The poncho is worn as a separate garment over a skirt or it can be attached to a skirt with laces. Fringe and other decoration can be added as desired. The skin drapes over the arms like sleeves but the side of the skin or sleeves are not sewed underneath. When worn the neck slit is side to side on the

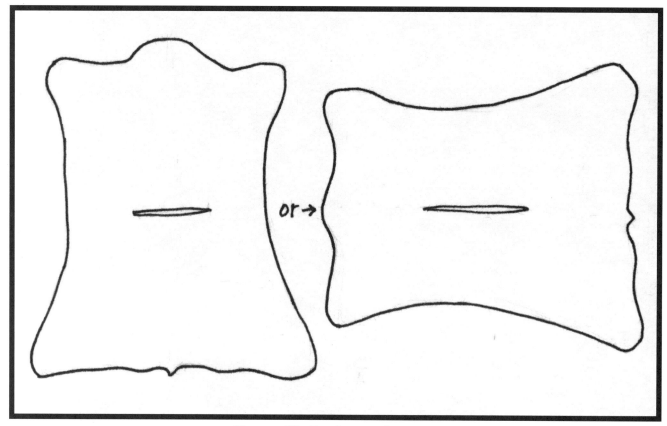

Figure 69. Basic poncho tops.

shoulders.

ROBES

MEN and WOMEN, Plains
To the Plains Indian a buffalo robe was their warmest and most protective piece of clothing; it was used for both bedding and clothing. The hair was normally left on for cold weather but some robes had the hair removed for mild weather.

A buffalo robe was usually made from two halves of a hide that were tanned separately and sewed together down the center. Red paint was painted on the seam to conceal the stitches.

Except in southern areas, the men usually wore their buffalo robes when appearing in public. The only difference between men's and women's buffalo robes was in the decoration.

Buffalo robes were worn in the winter with the hair next to body. Hats were not worn but the robes could be pulled up over their heads like hoods.

Blackfoot women were proud of their work and bragged about how many robes and teepee covers they could produce. Industrious workers could dress 25-30 buffalo robes in a season. Young girls were taught the skill and it was a valuable asset for them when looking for a husband.

MEN and WOMEN, Plains & Basin-Plateau
Robes were made from many different skins. Two deerskin or eighty ground squirrels would make a robe. Wolf, coyote, bear, marmot, muskrat, badger and other skins were used. Blackfoot and Bannock made rabbit skin robes and muskrat skin robes. Rabbit skins were used for children and babies.

RABBIT SKIN BLANKET OR ROBE

BASIN-PLATEAU

Communal rabbit drives were conducted more for the skins than for the meat. Working together natives sometimes killed hundreds of rabbits in one drive. Rabbit skin robes or blankets were often made by the men using a frame as a loom. The rabbit skins were cut spiral into long narrow strips, twisted into ropes and then woven together using sage brush bark, yucca, nettle, juniper, milkweed or dogbane cordage. Sometimes the strips of skin were wrapped around the cords for greater density, strength and warmth.

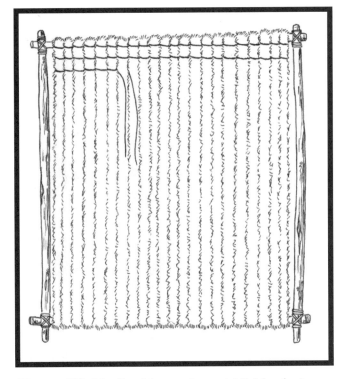

Figure 70. Vertical loom for rabbit blankets.

Figure 70 is an example of the type of loom used by Basin peoples to weave rabbit skin blankets. The twisted skin strips were wrapped around the bars and then a weft of buckskin or twisted fibers was twined in two interlocking strands through the rabbitskin warp. Other types of looms were used in other areas to make rabbit skin robes.

Figure 71. Rabbit skin blanket.

The rabbit skin blanket shown in *Figure 71* was constructed on a loom similar to the one shown in *Figure 70*. For this robe, the author used domestic rabbit hides cut spirally into strips, then twisted together and woven into a robe with yarn cordage.

Making a Rabbit Skin Blanket

To make a rabbit rope, start with a stretched, dry rabbit skin. Carefully scrape the fat and membrane off with a scraper as described in the brain tanning section or use a knife by scraping with the blade perpendicular to the skin. Care must be taken not to tear the thin skin. With a sharp knife and beginning at the bottom of the skin, cut spiral around the cased skin to make one long strip about l" wide (*Figure 72*).

Soak the strip in a bucket of warm water until it is soft and pliable. Take a small 2 or 3 ply cord about l/4" in diameter and about 6' long. Tie knots at both ends and then back twist one end

73

about 1/4" each turn. Wrap the flesh side in, leaving the hair side out. To do this, twist the rope and skin with one hand while feeding the fur strip on with the other.

After the strip of skin is wrapped, tuck the free end between the strands as was done to start the rope. Leave the rope stretched out to dry. As the rope dries brush or rub the fur periodically to fluff it up.

Another simple method of making rabbit ropes is to just twist the soaked fur strips together and not wrap them over a cord. To do this, tie the ends of a fur strip together with string, making a large fur loop. Link two or three of these fur loops together into a chain. Tie one end of the chain to a post and the other end to a spindle rope maker (see instructions below). Then using the rope maker twist the skins into a rabbit rope. The hair side usually tends to stay to the outside while the flesh side twists to the inside. Do not twist so tight that the skins buckle and break. The finished cord must be stretched between two points and both ends tied so that it cannot untwist while drying.

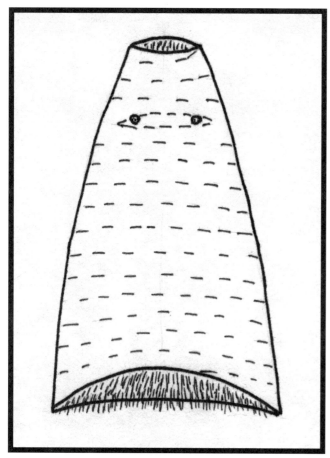

Figure 72. Method of cutting a rabbit hide into a long strip in preparation to making a rabbit robe.

of the cord and slip an end of the rabbit strip under one strand. Begin wrapping the rabbit strip around the cord (*Figure 73*) overlapping

To make a spindle for rope making cut a two inch diameter stick about 12-18 inches long. Flatten one end and drill a hole in the flattened end as shown in *Figure 74*. Carve notches on

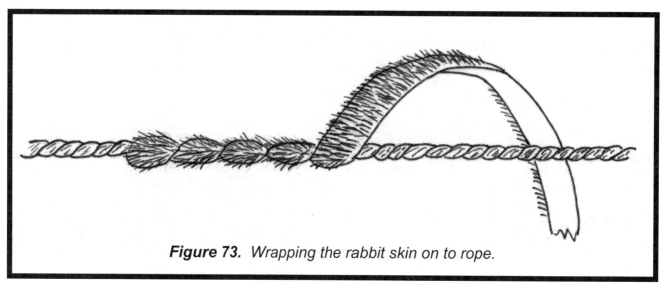

Figure 73. Wrapping the rabbit skin on to rope.

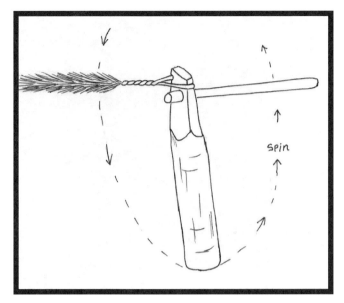

Figure 74. Wooden spindle for twisting rabbit strips into ropes. The ropes are then woven into blankets.

the edges of the flattened end to hold cordage that is to be twisted. Carve another stick as shown for a spindle or put a bolt in for the spindle.

This method of making rabbit ropes is faster than wrapping them around a cord, but the ropes are not as strong since there is no cord in the middle of the fur. Cordless ropes are suitable to be woven into rabbit blankets.

Next make a loom by lashing small poles together similar to the one shown in *Figure 70*. Wrap the rabbit ropes around the loom, tying each rope to the previous rope, until the desired size of blanket is obtained. Then using cordage, twine weave the rabbit ropes together. Start by looping a strand of cordage around the first rabbit rope and twisting the two strands a half turn together and lay in the next rope twisting the two strands a half turn again. Continue this until the edge is reached. Then either tie the strands off and start again at the opposite edge with another strand or just continue twinning back to the starting edge, twining back and forth until the blanket is completed. Tie in new strands of cordage as needed. When the blan-

ket is completed just unlash the poles and pull them out of the blanket.

In the Subarctic blankets were made from hare skins and were woven together in a different manner. The skins were cut spiral into long strips and twisted into furry cords similar to the method described above. A square or rectangular frame was made by tying four poles together and a selvage cord was laced inside the frame as a base to start weaving the hare skin strips. The twisted skin strips were looped through the selvage cord first and then looped through the previous row of hare skin strips. This was repeated back and forth until the blanket was the desired size. A wooden needle was used to pull the skins through the loops. It usually took about fifty skins to make one blanket.

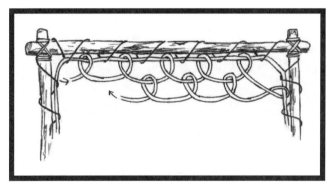

Figure 75. Subarctic method of weaving hareskin blankets.

The Subarctic method of weaving (series of loops) hare skins into blankets is shown above in *Figure 75*. The drawing shows the loops spread out for detail of construction but the actual loops would be pushed tighter.

A replicated rabbit or hare skin blanket made with either method above is simply dried raw hides and will soon attract clothes moths and dermistid beetles if it is not treated in some way. Once the blanket is constructed it could be tanned in an acid tan solution as described in the acid tan section of this book. Just run it through the tanning solution and then rinse as described and let it drip dry. There will be no

75

need to try to break it as it dries. Another way to protect it would be to try to smoke the blanket. This, however, could be a disaster if not carefully done because if the coals flared up it could easily burn and ruin the fur.

The blanket shown in *Figure 71* became infested with moths so to try to deter them the author did both; smoked it lightly and then soaked it in an acid tan solution. Aboriginal blankets no doubt were attacked by moths and other vermin and probably didn't last long. If a modern "abo" goes to all the trouble to make an authentic blanket he or she should consider "modern" ways to protect it. In addition to the above methods a person might also check with a museum for proper storage techniques to protect the blanket from insects and other pests.

SANDALS

There were many types of sandals made by early Native Americans. As mentioned earlier sandals were probably one of the most important items of clothing in the Southwest. They were also manufactured in the Basin, in California and other areas.

In *Figure 76* can be seen (a) a "two warp wickerwork" sandal from Tularosa cave New Mexico, while (b) shows the basic method by which sandals were woven. These sandals were made from twisted yucca leaves. A cord or warp is arranged in the shape and size of the sandal and twisted yucca leaves are wrapped around the outside of the warp in a figure eight manner to form the sole of the sandal. Cords are added for ankle and heel straps. Note that the cord that is used as the frame work is twisted at the toe and ties to the ankle cord. (From a sandal in the Chicago Field Museum collection # 260674.)

Figure 76 (c) is a California sandal made from rawhide; the sole has two layers of rawhide. It

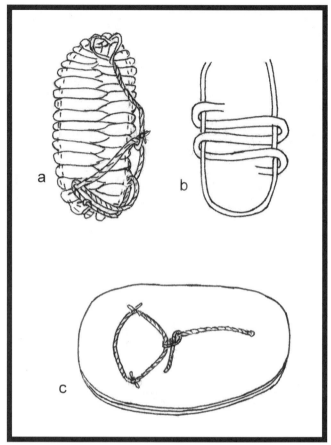

Figure 76. Fiber and rawhide sandals.

has straps for the ankle, heel and an adjustable strap going between the big and second toes. (From a sandal in the Department of Anthropology Smithsonian institution collection # 207604.)

The sandals shown in *Figure 77* were made similarly to some post contact sandals made by Southwest natives. These are light but comfortable to wear in warm weather. To make a pair use heavy stiff buckskin or rawhide from deer or elk. Make a pattern on paper by drawing around the foot and leaving a little extra space around the foot. Mark the location for one strap hole between the big toe and the second toe and then between the third and fourth toe. Draw tabs that extend out from each side of the sandal at the instep as shown in the photograph. Cut the pattern from the skin and punch holes for the straps in the places indicated. Cut two straps of soft buckskin and lace them into each sandal as shown. When wearing, insert the

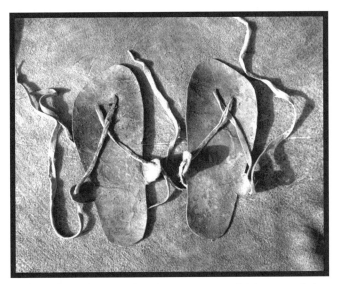

Figure 77. *Simple leather or rawhide sandals.*

second and third toes between the straps and use the loose ends to tie them.

SHIRTS

MEN'S, Plains

Early Plains shirts were made from two whole deer, elk or sheep skins and are called "binary shirts." They were sewn or tied together and worn like a poncho. Some were just sewn on the shoulders and the tops of the sleeves and sides were left open. They were fringed and occasionally the fringe could be used to make repairs by sewing or tying pieces together. The hind legs were often left on the shirts with hair and dew claws still attached, they hung down on the sides of the shirts. Two triangular flaps were made from the deer head skins and attached to the neck line in both the front and back of the shirt.

Winter shirts were made by folding small buffalo skins in half, cutting a neck slit and then lacing or tying the sides together. A similar shirt was made from two coyote skins. They were attached together, one in front and one in back, with the tails hanging down.

Buckskin shirts were not very common in the old days but were worn by members of honorary, or shirt-wearer, societies. They were made

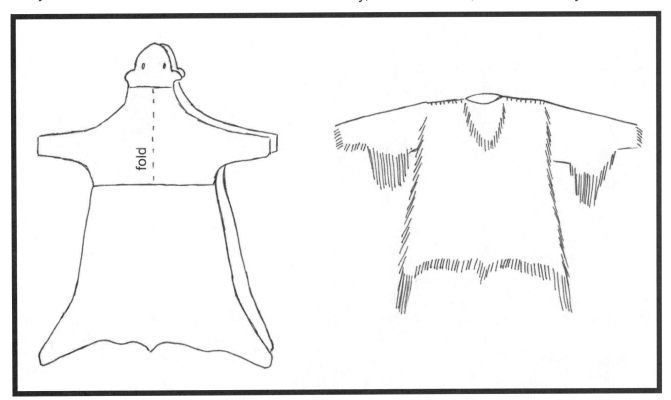

Figure 78. *Men's two skin buckskin shirt also known as a binary shirt.*

by older leaders and given to younger men who won membership in their societies. The shirt wearers were expected to act as leaders in battle as well as in everyday life and were to look after the welfare of their tribe. A shirt could be taken from a man if he disgraced these duties.

Making a men's Plains style shirt

Typically a man's shirt was made from two large skins as shown in *Figure 78*. To make this shirt obtain two

Figure 79. *Plains style binary shirt.*

tanned skins that are matched for size. Cut the skins straight across just below the front legs as shown. The two bottom portions become the front and back pieces and the two front quarter portions are used for the sleeves. Sew or lace the pieces together as shown in the drawings. The edges and ends may be cut into fringe as desired. If the skin that covered the heads is available, use it to make triangular or rectangular flaps and attach them to the neckline in front and back. If the head skin is not available cut flaps from any other pieces of skin.

If large or complete hides are not available then four smaller hides can be used to make the same shirt. The shirt in *Figure 79* was made that way. Two matching hides can be trimmed for the front and back pieces. Two matched, but smaller, hides are then used for the sleeves. They should be folded along the back bone and trimmed to the proper length and shape for the sleeve. Sew, lace or tie all pieces of leather together to complete the shirt as shown in the drawing and in *Figure 79*. Triangular flaps can be added at the neck and all edges of the skin can be cut into fringe as shown.

Decorations

In addition to fringe being cut into most free edges of buckskin shirts there are several other types of decorations that can be added to a man's Plains style shirt:

Bands of quillwork or beadwork can be added to the shirts over the shoulders and on the sleeves. On early shirts these bands were often narrow and were placed vertically over the shoulders; they were not always put on the arms. Later shirts were made with wider bands and they began to put them on at an angle over the shoulders as shown in *Figure 80*. They also began to put them on the arms of the shirt.

Bunches of hair (wrapped with quills) tied to the seams. Weasel skins or other skin strips tied to the seams of the shirt if desired.

Quillwork or beadwork on the triangular neck flap.

The Crow used quilled strips on the shoulders and sleeves of their shirts. Also they often put large quilled rosettes on both the front and back of the shirt.

Members of the Cheyenne Nation used hair

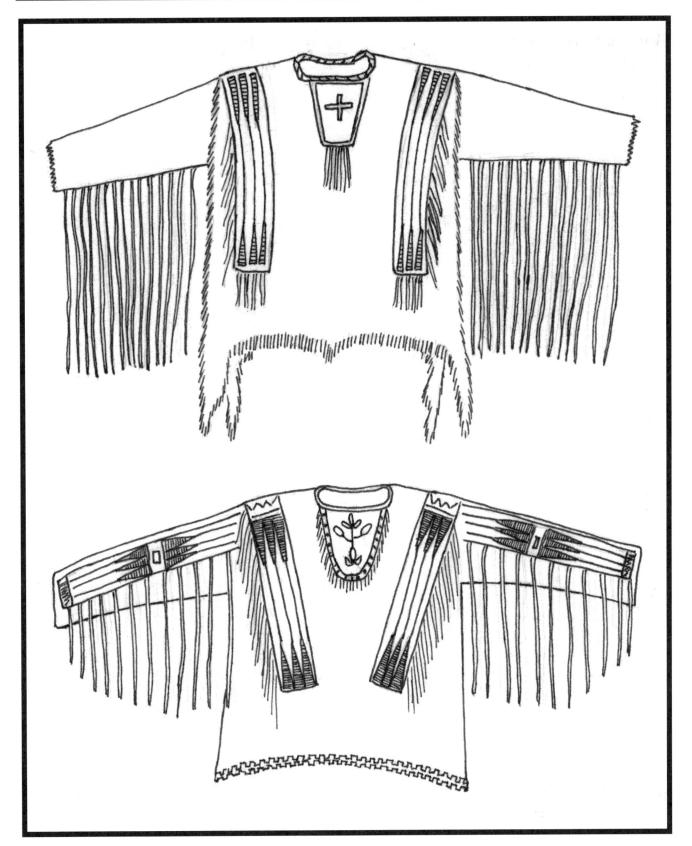

Figure 80. *Drawing of an early style shirt (top) and a later style (bottom). The early style is decorated with fringe and quillwork on the bibs and over the shoulders, while just the later style shirt has quillwork on the sleeves.*

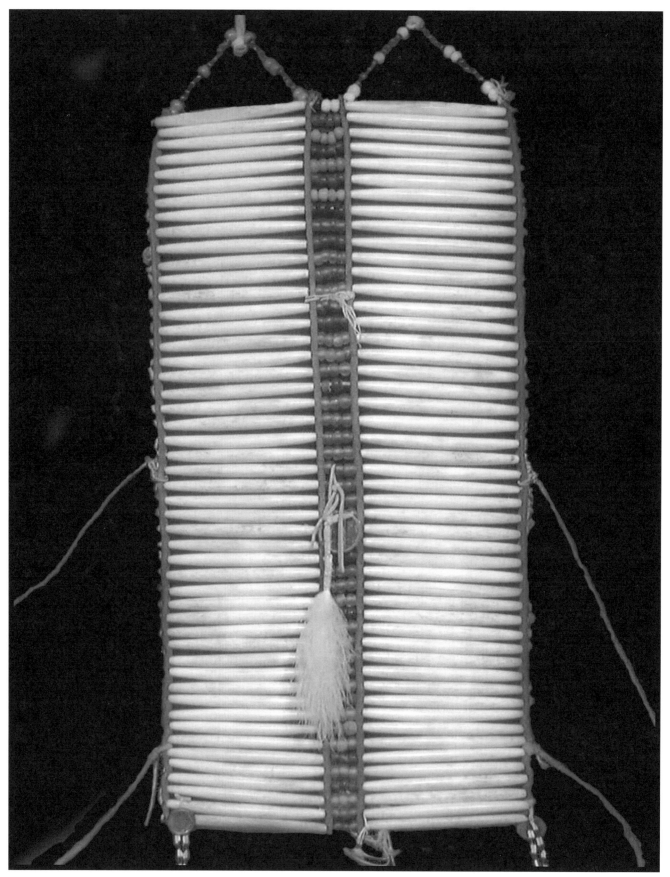

Figure 81. Man's breast plate, Sioux.

locks and quilled strips on the arms and shoulders.

Kiowa and Comanche men used the quilled strips similar to other Plains groups. They sometimes decorated their shirts with hair locks, but usually used long buckskin thongs instead. These long fringes were only on the shoulders and elbows leaving the rest of the fringe short. Decoration also included large amounts of pigment of yellow, green, red or blue and a flicker feather medicine bundle on the right shoulder.

BREASTPLATE

MEN, Plains Indians

The breastplate was used to protect the wearer from wounds due to arrows and lance and actually worked to good effect, depending upon distance, with fire arms. *Figure 81* illustrates an old type breastplate made from bone "Hair Pipes" and a harness of buckskin strips. Beads are early type, and the feather tufts are Golden Eagle. Used by permission from the Native American Collection, Gordon B. Olson Library, Minot State University, Minot, North Dakota. Photographed by Joseph Jastrzembski.

SLIPPERS

Figure 82 is a slipper from the Mammoth Cave, Catalog # 1625. It is a twined slipper used by the Southeast and Woodland peoples and this drawing was done by Joan Miller of Michigan. This slipper is currently curated at Mammoth Cave, Kentucky. This intact slipper is an exceptional example of aboriginal craftsmanship. The only visible damage is in the heel area where the warp strands appear to have been broken by the strain of wear. A two ply cord was laced through the slipper body to repair the damage and it also appears to have been broken by wear. Drawing and the following section courtesy of Joan Miller.

Baskets for Your Feet by Joan Miller

"I have been caving for several years in the Fisher Ridge Cave System in Kentucky. Discovered in 1981, it is now the fourth longest cave in the United States. Several miles from the only natural entrance to the cave, we discovered footprints that none of us made. The prints were in a nice high, dry passage above the level that periodically floods. Dr. Patty Jo Watson, a cave archaeologist from the University Of Washington in Missouri, examined the footprints and removed some burned cane torch pieces from the area for carbon dating. The resulting dates put Woodland culture exploration of Fisher Ridge Cave at 1375 B.C. to 2050 B.C. According to Dr. Watson, the footprints were made by two adults and two younger people wearing twined slippers.

"Slippers and slipper prints have been found along passageways miles from the entrances to these southeastern caves. The Woodland people of the American Southeast searched these limestone caves to mine cave salts. Limestone which litters cave floors is extremely abrasive to the soles of these fabric shoes. When the slipper would no longer stay on the foot, it was left in the isolation of the cave environment and so preserved for centuries. I saw two slippers in situ, clearly left where the next caver through the passage was likely to step on it. A slipper left along the path could cushion the next caver's step.

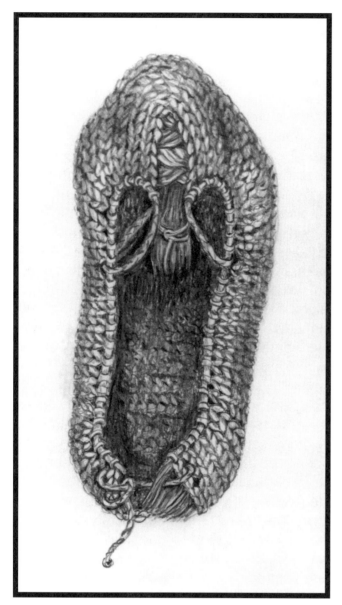

Figure 82. *Southeastern twined slipper.*

archaeology class and Dr. Watson, the instructor for the class, encouraged me to tackle the slipper replication puzzle. So began a four year pursuit to understand the twining process originally used to produce the Woodland slippers. This quest has led me into museum storerooms to examine curated slippers, the depths of caves to look at the fragmented pieces and deep inside my own creative instincts.

"The Woodland twiners used *Eryngium yuccafolium* (Rattlesnake Master) to make slippers. I use common jute cord because rattlesnake master is very rarely found in the Southeast today."

Making the Slippers
"Cut the number of warp strands that will be needed. As a general rule slippers take two strands more than the foot size. But some experimentation may be required to get the right number of strands. For a Size 8 foot start with ten warp strands. I suggest that a heavier jute be used for the outer selvage edge warp strand, but two or three regular sized strands can also be held together and used as the selvage edge warp strand. The slipper is twinned flat. The curve around the heel and toe is created by pulling the warp strands through the finished flat piece once the desired size is reached. The flat mat should be about an inch wider than your foot on both sides and about an inch and a half longer than the foot.

"Twined slippers are perhaps the most charming and personal of the cave artifacts. You can still see a muddy print of the original owner's foot inside most slippers. I think of the slippers as "baskets for your feet" because the earliest twined goods were basket like containers. What makes this design surprisingly unique is the one step taken to further the process and make the baskets fit snugly over the toes and around the heel!

"No one had ever replicated a Woodland twined slipper. In the summer of 1986 I took a cave

"The weft strand that will be used to begin the piece should be cut about six to eight feet long. Loop the center of the weft strand around the first warp strand which will be the selvage edge. Then with the thumb and index finger of the right hand twist the weft strands together, one half turn, moving the back strand over the front strand (a counter clockwise turn). Then lay the next warp strand between the wefts and again twist the weft around it, back strand over front strand as before. Add warp strands in succession and twist the weft around them until all the

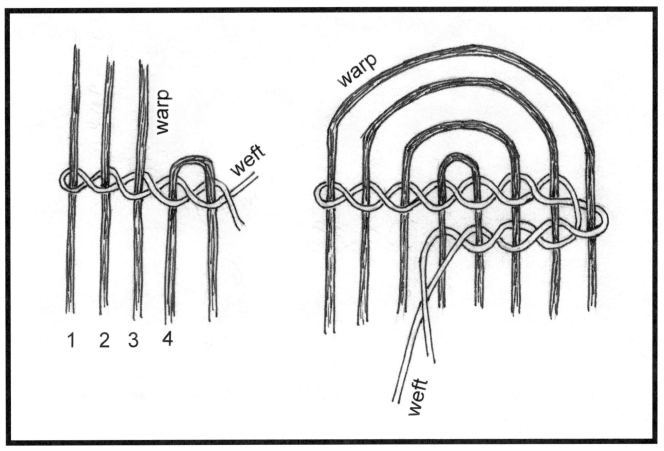

Figure 83. Method of twining slippers (drawing is spread out for clarity).

pieces of warp have been incorporated. Next fold down the last piece of warp and twist the weft around it as before (See *Figure 83*). Continue folding down warp strands and twisting the weft around them until the last strand is reached, which again is the selvage edge.

"When the edge is reached lay the last warp strand between the wefts as before and bring the back strand around to the front to begin twisting back to the other side. Now here is the secret: "With the left hand twist the two weft fibers, front strand over the back strand (a counter clockwise turn) on just the first warp fiber then lay in the second fiber and begin twisting the other way, the back weft strand over the front weft strand (clockwise)." Continue laying in strands and twisting, back strand over front strand, as the work progresses from right to left. Twisting with the left hand will be the mirror image of twisting with the right hand and the twist

will be in the opposite direction creating the chevron pattern in the weave.

"Again when the left edge is reached bend the fibers over to the front, switch to twisting with the right hand, the first twist will be front over back (clockwise), then insert the second fiber and twist the wefts, the back one over the front one(counter clockwise), proceeding as before from left to right, inserting warp strands and twisting wefts strands, back ones over front ones in a counter clockwise twist. With a little practice this will become second nature.

"Untangle the weft strands from the warp strands every few twists, try to make the twists consistent and compact each row as tightly as possible against the previous row.

"Adding weft when the previous weft strands have been incorporated into the piece is simple.

"When only about two inches of weft is left, loop a new weft strand around the last warp strand that was twine twisted and continue twisting as before. When arriving back to where the weft is protruding, place each old weft strand down alongside a warp strand and twine twist the new weft around the two. After a few rows the old weft ends will have disappeared into the fabric of the slipper and will not be detectable.

Figure 84. This is a pair of slippers made by the author using Joan Miller's techniques. The small slipper was made by Joan.

"When the flat mat is the proper size, finish the twining in the center and tie the two weft strands in a bundle with a slip knot. Then pull the warp strands to create the curve of the heel, begin with the middle warp strand pulling it gently toward the toe of the flat piece. This strand should be pulled until it disappears into the fabric. Each warp strand is then pulled, creating a curve of open twining around the heel. These strands can be adjusted from either end of the fabric.

"To pull the warp strands for the toe, follow the same procedure, only begin from the outside with the selvage edge first. Gently curve and mold the edge of the flat piece over the toe as the warps are pulled. Once the toe area is curved up properly, the selvage warp strands are looped back through themselves at the edges about eight or ten twists back from the last row completed.

"After the warp strands are looped back through pull them up with all the other warp strands to begin the braid over the toe. This is done like a French braid, start at the tip of the toe. Pick up two strands from the middle and two strands on each side of them. Begin a normal three strand braid with these three elements but pick up and add one more warp strand each time the braid proceeds from side to side. After all the warp strands have been incorporated into the braid, continue braiding for a couple of inches, take one warp strand and wrap it several times

"around the others and secure it with a slip knot. Then cut the protruding warp strands off about an inch past the slip knot. Make sure, that as the braid is made, the two bundled up weft strands end up inside the slipper. The slipper is now finished.

"There are no knots, no loose ends and no elements that cannot adjust to the foot that sets this slipper in motion. I've worn my pair of slippers many times, while giving demonstrations of their construction and they fit amazingly well. They stay on my feet even when I run, they don't slip off the heel and they feel quite comfortable."

WAMPUM - HEAD BANDS AND BELTS

White beads or "Wampum" were made from periwinkle (welk) shells by the Eastern Indians. Black or purple beads were made from Quahog shells. The beads were drilled with stone bits and shaped by sanding and woven in patterns on cordage to make bracelets, collars, headbands, belts and other decorations. The belt patterns were often symbolic and served as mnemonic devices to record treaties and other tribal records.

OTHER ITEMS

Cradleboards

Although not clothing the cradleboard was an important article in the life of infants and their mothers. Cradles were used in most cultural areas except in the far north in the cold regions and in the extreme heat of the southern regions. In the Arctic the babies were carried inside the mothers parka, and in the Subarctic babies were carried inside a bag of moss. In the south near the Mexican border, babies were carried in a small hammock on their mothers hip.

The style of cradles varied from one area to another, but were basically a framework of sticks or boards with a buckskin or cloth cover into which the baby could be laced and secured. The baby was laced into its cradle while being carried about during the day and was left in it at night. In addition to physically protecting the baby, the cradles insured the total well-being of the child by its materials and decorations.

WEARING BUCKSKIN 365 DAYS A YEAR

By Matt McMahon

Who says buckskin clothing is not attractive? *Figure 85* is an example of the dress of a growing number of individuals who wear buckskin clothing on a year round basis. There is a certain romantic naturalness in wearing this type of clothing. Whether it be authentic traditional style or clothing of a person's own design, it strips away modern fad and fashion and seems to transform the wearer back in time to a simpler world.

Most people who make buckskin clothing probably wear it only a few times a year - on special occasions, such as at traditional rendezvous re-enacting our coun-try's early history or at other similar occasions. A few but growing number of individuals have

been tanning skins, making their own clothing, and wearing it on a daily basis throughout the year. Their clothing is both attractive and functional. It is usually of their own design and not styled purely traditional or modern; they have borrowed design elements from both worlds.

Much can be learned about how buckskin clothing functions on a daily basis, the type of clothing to make, and how to care for it from these people. The following is a quote from a letter from Matt McMahon, one such person. At the time of his writing, during the early 1990s, Matt and his family had been living in the woods for several years and making their living from primitive skills. His letter could have been writ-

85

ten during the 1890s:

"So here is a few notes about our lifestyle in buckskin as you requested. My wife and I and our two daughters, four and one, all wear a combination of wool and buckskin 365 days a year. As we are some of very few people who do this, we have learned much about the properties and long term maintenance of buckskin that only long steady wear can reveal. We wear our buckskins in realistic activities such as hunting, trapping and gathering as well as around our camp. We cannot imagine another garment more appropriate for long-wearing in a demanding environment and I think the Natives and mountain men would agree. Besides it is the only fabric available from the woods unless you like wearing cedar bark!

"Wool (spun or felted) is the other fabric whose properties compliment buckskin overgarments. With wool sweaters and long johns (100% wool, no cotton!) under buckskin, you can exploit the properties of both fabrics. The wool next to the skin for warmth and wicking and the buckskin as the windproof durable shell. And, there is nothing more disgusting than 100% soaked buckskin in the rain, 40% maybe, even 60% maybe? But totally soaked buckskin is a real drag! I wear an oil-skin coat or heavy capote in rain. And, like a lot of Natives, I don't go out in downpours as my sinewed bows and arrows are too valuable to get wet!

"We have both summer and winter sets of 'skins. My summer shirt is sleeveless and very thin, made from antelope. Antelope and goat are great for light skins. These garments are not stitched too tight, but are loosely laced and tied to allow plenty of air circulation. My shirt is cool even to 90 degrees plus, after which I'll be in a loincloth. The light shirt dries very quickly after washing. My winter shirt is like a storm shield. It is long sleeved and goes down well over my rear. It is made from heavy winter weight big mule deer bucks. Some exceptional big buck-

skins are as thick as moose skins. This garment is cut big to go over woolens and all seams are sewn (laced) up tight with all seams welted. Neither fifty mile per hour winds, nor barbed wire can make it through this armor! I can crash through thorn thickets that stop typically dressed folks.

"My wife and girls also have summer and winter weight dresses. Short and loose laced for summer, full-length, sleeved, welted big skins for winter. We all wear leggings too but I've taken a liking to my heavy skin pants. Maybe it's the white man in me, but I like to cover my backside!

"All pants break stitching at the crotch so make sure to use strong laces. We always presoak and stretch buckskin lace to prevent loosening of seams later. When sewing skins always keep awl holes well into the hide and away from edges to prevent stretching and breaking of holes after hard use. A good strong pre-stretched lace, with small awl holes far from the edge and sewn in welt make for long wearing seams. Even with the inevitable repairs, I prefer my pants over leggings in all but the hottest of weather. This is because my hips are skinny and the belt of the leggings cuts into the skin. With my pants, the weight is evenly distributed around my waist. This doesn't seem to bother my wife as she prefers leggings. However, she also has nicely padded hips to hang them on! It is strictly a matter of choice.

"Many of our garments are dyed with a natural fir bark or alder bark solution - lots of green bark with enough water to cover it, boiled 6-8 hours yields a rust/brown liquid. Cool the liquid, soak the garments several hours, rinse and dry and they will be a dark rust color. The color of smoked skins is another subject. It doesn't matter how dark the smoke color is, it always fades after washing until it is white. White is my least favorite color for working clothes! Few people ever reach this stage with buckskin as they don't wash and wear it enough. You may manage to keep color in a pouch or hat or that twice a year worn 'costume,' but if you wear buckskin every day and wash it once a week, that's 52 washings a year. Even after 20 washes your skins are close to white. Also, if you really wear them, you get stains from soil, campfire and whatever and a stiff brush scrubbing is the only way to get those stains out. As you scrub you wash away the smoke color. In other words the harder you work, the quicker they fade! Of course you can always re-smoke for looks but there is no need for function and re-smoking is added maintenance that you don't need!

"Constant attention to careful washing, drying and repair and maintenance to laced or stitched seams are the main concern for long term wear of buckskins. Also bear in mind that the dirt and soil build up on clothing affects its warmth and waterproofness. Dirt, soil and body oils clog the pores of the buckskin and when flat and oily it sheds water better but loses some of its warmth. Clean and fluffy buckskin or wool is always warmer, but gets wet quicker too. However you choose to wear skins, when you start wearing them every day you gotta keep your eyes on them. It's the old 'stitch in time saves nine'."

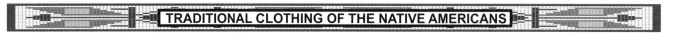

NOTES

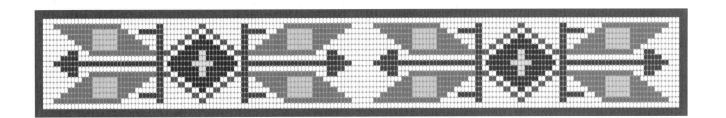

SECTION II

BUCKSKIN TODAY

While the preceding sections contained ideas for making authentic traditional clothing, this chapter provides ideas for making both "period like" and modern clothing from buckskin. Most of the clothing items and ideas described in this section were submitted to the author by others and they cover a range of ideas. As will be mentioned in a later section of this book, just about anything made from fabric can also be made from leather or buckskin. Patterns for fabric clothing can also be used to make buckskin clothing (see the section "Tips For Sewing"). Many people don't need patterns to make attractive buckskin clothing and a person is limited only by his imagination and creativity. The following are descriptions of these kinds of clothing items.

The sleeveless buckskin tunic top, shown in *Figure 86*, is not really an authentic traditional style nor is it a modern style, but is a generic top resembling what a period tunic top may have looked like. Some Native groups may have made tunic tops similar to this when they wore tops with their skirts.

Two small hides were cut similar to a tank top. The pieces were tied together at the shoulders and sides with a few strips of buckskin. The slit in the front had holes punched in either side and a strip of buckskin added with which to lace it. The laces can be loosened in hot weather and adjusted for the desired fit.

This top was purposely made rough and primi-

Buckskin Tunic Top

Figure 86

Figure 87. Buckskin pants.

90

tive looking. None of the holes were sewn closed to give it a more traditional look.

Buckskin Pants

Figure 87 illustrates a pair of buckskin pants that were made by Mike Sullivan. Buckskin pants can be made by using a good fitting pair of pants as a pattern. Modern style pants or period (1800's) pants can be made this way. Also there are a number of patterns available from leather craft suppliers.

Buckskin Dress

Figure 88. Buckskin dress.

A buckskin dress made by Mike Sullivan for his daughter is shown in *Figure 88*. This is a basic side fold dress with an insert of fur placed over the right shoulder.

Buckskin Skirt and Top

Figure 89. Buckskin skirt and top.

Julie Newnam shows a buckskin skirt and top she made in *Figure 89*. This is an excellent example of an article that shares both modern and traditional style. The skirt is made with two deerskins trimmed roughly to shape leaving the bottom of the skins in their natural shape. The two skirt pieces are tied together along the sides with buckskin laces and the sides were fringed. The sides of the skirt are open at the top so that it may be slipped on over the hips. It is then closed and held with a buckskin belt. The top is made with two pieces of skin. The back piece goes from the waistline up over the shoulders and is stitched, using a running stitch, with buckskin thongs to the front piece; this forms a yoke above the bustline. The front and back pieces are tied together at the sides with buckskin thongs.

The neck hole was cut, a small portion folded over and stitched with buckskin thongs in a running stitch.

Buckskin Neck Tie

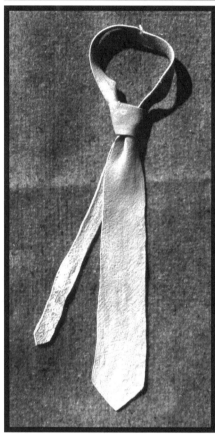

Figure 90. Buckskin neck tie.

As a novelty, a few years ago the author decided to make a buckskin neck tie; this is shown in *Figure 90*. A standard tie was used for a pattern. It was laid down on the center of a buckskin and traced lightly with a pencil. It was then cut out with scissors and the outside edge left raw. The tie was longer than the skin so two pieces were cut out and sewn together. The front (fatter end) of the tie was made from the longest piece so the joint, with the smallest piece, is about 1/3 of the length of the narrow end. The tie can be worn with either the flesh side or the hair side out as it looks good either way. The author occasionally wears this tie to church and it almost always nets a compliment

or some questions. Buckskin is thicker than regular tie material and is somewhat difficult to tie in a good knot, so an alternative method could be to tie a shorter buckskin tie to a clip-on tie clip. This might be the ultimate combination of primitive and modern dress! Wearing a buckskin tie is a subtle way to put a little primitive personality into modern dress clothing!

Modern Wrap Skirts

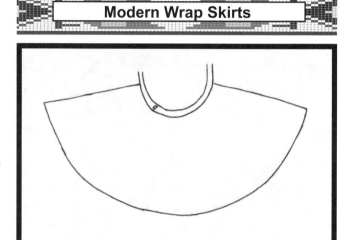

Figure 91. Modern wrap skirts. Top, wrap skirt laid out flat showing pattern. Bottom, beaded and fringed wrap skirt.

The basic pattern of a wrap skirt is shown above. The pattern is part of a circle as shown and is not a rectangle. The top of the skirt and waist band should be long enough to go around the waist one and a half times. A full skirt would be close to a half circle as shown in the first drawing. A less full skirt would be a smaller part of a circle. Adjust the pattern to the desired length and style and make the skirt from old material to test the fit before cutting the skirt from buckskin. Several hides may need to be trimmed and sewed together to make the skirt. Orient the hides so that the line of the backbones radiate out from the waist band. Extend the waist band or add either buckskin straps or cords for ties. The skirt can be simply wrapped around the body and the straps tied or a slit can be cut in the waist band, as shown in *Figure 91*. One strap is slipped through the slit and then the straps are wrapped around the waist and tied. The skirt can be left plain or decorated to taste with fringe and/or beads.

The second drawing in *Figure 91* is of a buckskin wrap skirt seen at a mountain man rendezvous. The skirt was cut in a smooth curve from the waist to the hem. The edge was cut into fringe and a beaded strip was added along the edge. Two buttons were placed on the waist

band for attachment. To make this skirt lay the pattern out like the pattern above and then cut a sweeping curve from each outside edge to the hem. It may take some experimentation to get the desired effect.

One lady suggested that a nice buckskin skirt could be made with buckskin laces as a closure instead of buttons or zippers. Use a gored skirt pattern and put holes and a buckskin lace in place of the zipper. The lacing slit could be in the back, front or side as desired, but would need to open far enough to pass over the fullest part of the hips.

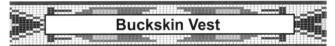

Buckskin Vest

Dorraine Pool made the buckskin vest shown in *Figure 92*. This is a very attractive vest and can be worn with everyday clothing, western wear or mountain man gear. Her husband tanned the hides and she designed the pattern. The diagram in *Figure 93* shows the shape of the pattern pieces. It is stitched with buckskin

Figure 92. Buckskin vest.

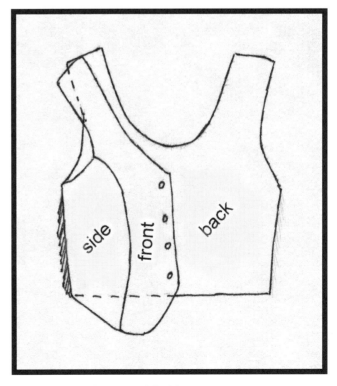

Figure 93. Vest pattern

strips and has fringe with beads, bones and quills attached. The front closure buttons are made from antler. Dorraine whip stitched around the neck opening.

The drawing in *Figure 93* shows the pattern pieces and their relationship to each other. The back is one piece and the side and front pieces are the same for either right or left sides.

Buckskin Intimates

Authentic traditional style dresses, and tops sometimes have gaps between the ties and are usually open under the sleeves, sometimes allowing underwear and/or skin to show through. If a woman wants to wear authentic traditional

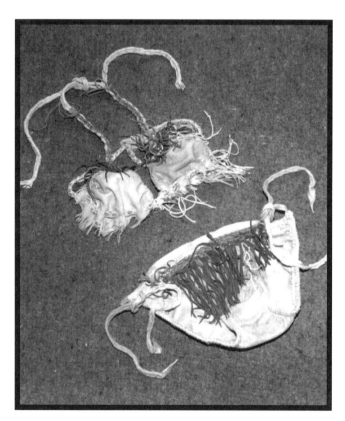

Figure 94. Made by Dorraine Pool, this a buckskin bikini made from the "Bikini Bathing Suits," pattern available from Tandy Leather Company. Dorraine followed the pattern for the basic bathing suit but modified the straps using her strip rolling process. (See Strip Rolling instructions in the next section.)

styles but does not want to go without underwear as the natives did or allow modern underwear to show through, a good alternative is to make underwear from soft buckskin.

There are bra and panty patterns that can be used or the creative craftsperson may want to design her own. Someone once said "It takes an engineer to design a bra!" but a pattern can be taken from a commercial bra as demonstrated by this project submitted by Dorraine Pool. (See Dorraine's buckskin bikini, left, for ideas to make buckskin panties.)

Referring to *Figure 95*, Dorraine reports, "This is a buckskin bra I made by taking a pattern from the commercial bra shown in the inset to the left. I was fortunate to have three different colors of antelope buckskin, light, medium and dark brown. This gave it a great look.

"I have fun lacing and inventing different ways of putting things together and I felt honored and was so excited to be asked to help with this project. It is thrilling to be able to do something that is challenging and I especially liked getting to use Evard's buckskin. For this project a person can adapt any bra and should use their favorite and most comfortable one. I used an underwire style with lace on the top half of the cups, size 34B. I made the pattern by first making a paper pattern then a cloth pattern then finally transferring it to buckskin.

" To make the paper pattern pin the article directly to the paper and trace each piece separately, add about 1/4 inch seam allowance. Be sure to mark each pattern piece with the pertinent information such as RIGHT SIDE - LEFT SIDE - TOP - BOTTOM - SEAM ALLOWANCE - ETC. Next pin the paper pattern together, overlapping the seam allowances and compare carefully to the original garment. Make adjustments as needed. Make sure the seams match. Since buckskin does not stretch as much as the bra fabric, cut the ends where the bra will join in

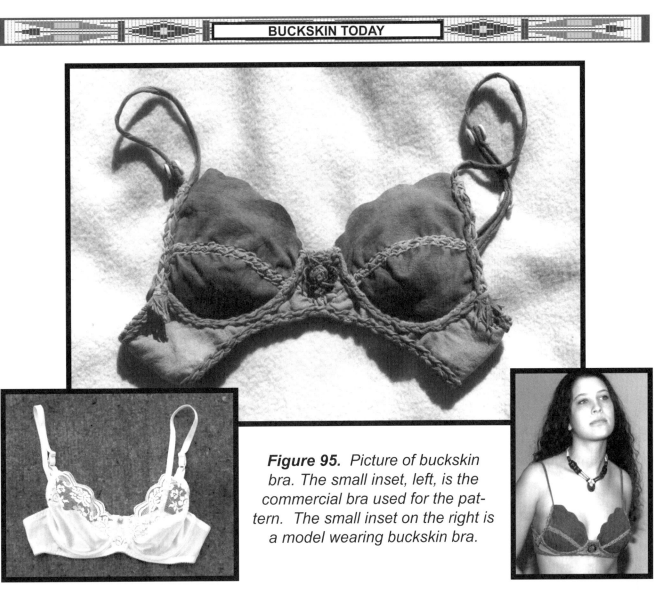

Figure 95. Picture of buckskin bra. The small inset, left, is the commercial bra used for the pattern. The small inset on the right is a model wearing buckskin bra.

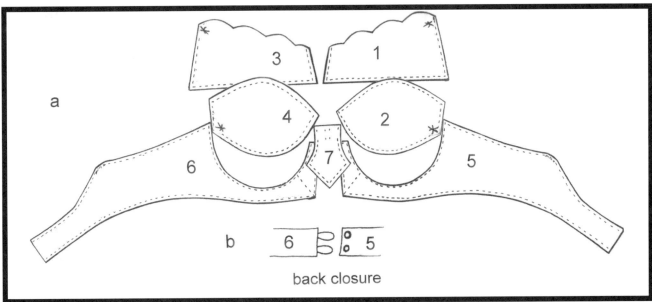

back closure

Figure 96. Finished pattern Dorraine made from the commercial bra. (a) How pieces fit together and (b) Back closure.

the back a little longer than the original article. It can be cut shorter if needed after it is all laced together. Start over if needed because time spent adjusting the paper pattern will save time in the long run. Once the paper pattern and original article are compared and no more adjustments are needed proceed to the muslin.

"Pin the paper pattern to the muslin, cut it out and pin the article together. The muslin contours better than paper so again compare to the original. Make adjustments as needed.

"Select soft thin buckskin. Lay the material pattern on the buckskin, making certain that there is enough buckskin for all of the pieces and pin carefully in the seam allowances. Try not to put too many extra holes in the buckskin. Cut out the pieces and leave one pin attaching each pattern to the piece until ready to assemble the final article.

"When assembling the bra, lace the pieces together with thin strips of buckskin using the decorative stitches and pieces of "rolled strips" as explained at the end of this article. Begin assembly by sewing the top pieces of the cups #1 and #3 to the bottom pieces #2 and #4. Next sew the bottom pieces of the bra #6 and #5 together, and then sew piece #7 into the inside to strengthen the center of the bra.

"The seam sewing the cups to the bottom part of the bra is done differently since it will need to provide support similar to an *underwire*. Instead of overlapping, put the two raw edges together as shown in *Figure 97d*, and lace them together with the crisscross cross stitch. Next, using a straight stitch, lace one of the rolled strips to the same seam to give it a little extra support and to keep the buckskin from stretching out of shape. When lacing the rolled strip to the *underwire* seam, try to use the same holes already cut as much as possible.

"The next step is to finish around the edges of

pieces #5 and #6, first with a straight stitch, followed by a crisscross cross stitch. A second option is to finish the outer edges by lacing a rolled strip to the edge with a straight stitch and follow with a crisscross cross stitch. I laced rolled strips to the outer edge of the bra which gave it a lacier look and also additional strength. This lacing should also be done to the small piece between the cups. I did not do any finish to the scalloped edge of the top of the cups.

"Then attach the shoulder straps. Prepare them by cutting two buckskin straps that are 3/4 inch wide and are long enough for the shoulder straps with room for adjustment. Roll these two straps, as explained in the strip rolling section below. After rolling soak them in water for about 15 minutes, squeeze out the excess water and stretch them out on a flat surface with thumb tacks on either end and leave them to dry.

"To attach the straps make incisions on the arm side at the bottom and outer edge of each cup, use the asterisks (*) on the pattern as a guide. Take the end of one shoulder strap and start by lacing through the bottom holes three or four times. Then using the straight stitch, followed by the crisscross cross stitch, sew the strap to the edge of the cup. Continue to the top of the cup and lace through the top incisions three or four times and tie the laces off. Do the other side.

"To attach the straps to the back of the bra take two short buckskin strips and lace them to the back of pieces #5 and #6 making loops at the point where the straps attach. Now put the ends of the shoulder straps through the loops, adjust to the length needed and either tie off with lacing or put bone buttons on to make the straps adjustable.

"To make the back closure, take two more short strips of buckskin and attach them to the end of piece #6 in loops just like above. Attach bone buttons to the end of Piece #5 to complete the back closure (see *Figure 96b*).

"The final thing to do is make sure all the ends of the lacing are tied off and tucked into the existing lacing. I added a small rose on the front of the bra for decoration. I did this by taking one of the rolled strips and made sort of a pinwheel and laced it together so that it laid more or less flat. Then I added a few beads.

STRIP ROLLING PROCESS

"For the strip rolling process cut buckskin strips that are 1/2 inch wide and as long as the buckskin pieces allow. As mentioned earlier cut two pieces that are 3/4 inches wide for the bra shoulder straps. Now take the strips and cut a series of small slits down the middle of the strip. To do this use scissors. Start at one end of the strip,

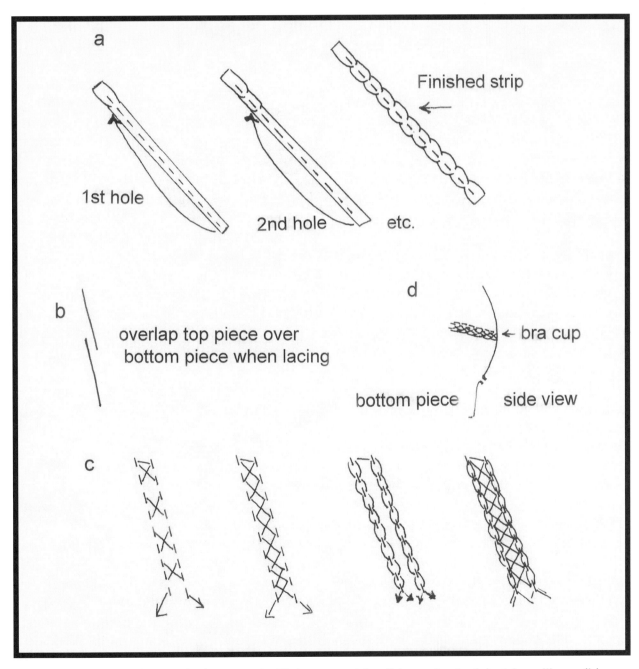

Figure 97. *Strip rolling technique and stitches used for this project: (a) strip rolling, (b) seam overlap, (c) Lacing techniques, and (d)* underwire *seam attachment.*

fold it over and just barely snip the middle of the fold with the tip of the scissors. Leave a small gap, fold the strip over and snip again. The bigger the cut the longer the slit will be. Continue to the end of the strip (see *Figure 97a*). Now take the strip by one end and bring the other end up through the first hole from the top and pull it through until it is tight. Continue pulling the end through each successive hole in the same manner until the end is reached. This produces a strip of buckskin that is rolled.

LACING TECHNIQUES USED

"Assembly of this article was done by lacing the pieces together with strips of buckskin. First cut strips of buckskin approximately 1/8 of an inch thick. Cut around the edges of scrap pieces right to the center making long strips of lacing. These should be wetted, stretched out longer and allowed to dry before use.

"Before lacing pieces together, make small incisions at the seam line with a seam ripper. Start with one side and by carefully poking the seam ripper through the buckskin to make the cuts. They should be about 1/4 of an inch apart following the seam line. Use the seam ripper as a ruler, just mentally mark where 1/4 inch is on the ripper and measure the distance between incisions with it. Now take the piece that attaches to the piece that the holes were just punched in and pin the two pieces together. Again pin only on the outer edges. Punch the first hole in one end through the incision of the first piece and then mark the remaining hole locations. Separate the two pieces and punch the remaining slits in the second piece.

"The following lacing technique applies to lacing all pieces together except for the underwire seams that were explained earlier: Take the two pieces that will be laced together and overlap the seam allowances so that the row of slits on one piece lines up with the cut edge of the other piece (see *Figure 97b*). Then insert a piece of lacing through both first holes and pull it in until it is divided in half. Now take one of the laces and cross it over and insert it down through the second hole of the other piece being laced together. Again cross it back and bring it up through the third hole of the first piece. Use a pair of jewelers pointed tweezers to pull the lacing through with. Just insert the tweezers through the holes, grab the lace with them and pull it through the hole. Continue this crisscross cross lacing technique to the end of the seam. Go back and get the other half of the lace and repeat the same procedure (see *Figure 97c*).

"Next lace both pieces of lace in the same manner back in the opposite direction to where the lacing first started. The next step of this decorative lacing procedure is to take each half of the lace and run it in a straight stitch (running stitch), one on one side of the seam and one on the other side (see *Figure 97c*). The rolled strips can be attached at the same time this last straight stitch is applied to the piece.

"In conclusion; using the techniques described in this section one can take any article of clothing and convert it first to a paper pattern, then to material and finally to buckskin."

Another simple bra idea comes from an article in the October 25, 1983 issue of Woman's Day Magazine. This article describes how to make a bra from a handkerchief; by substituting buckskin, a simple buckskin bra may be made.

First cut a square piece of buckskin that measures 8 inches by 8 inches. Cut this in half diagonally forming two triangles that are 8 inches by 8 inches by 11 3/4 inches. The size, of course, may need to be adjusted according to the bra size desired. Gather and sew the 11 3/4 inch sides to a length of 7 1/2 inches; this produces a piece 8" x 8" x a gathered 7 1/2" - the gathered side forms the bottom of the cup. Sew a small strip of buckskin to the cups to hold them together in the center so the corners just touch.

Add buckskin straps that tie in the back and straps to tie around the neck.

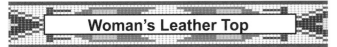
Woman's Leather Top

The woman's leather top, shown in *Figure 98*, was designed by Molly Miller. This simple woman's top is not an authentic traditional article of clothing but is similar to a halter top. It is made from buckskin and there is no specific pattern. Cut the buckskin large enough to cover the chest in the general shape as shown in the *Figure* (the back is left bare). The design can be varied to suit personal taste. Fringe and other decoration can be added if desired or it can be left plain. Shoulder straps are added so that they cross over in the back. The strap coming from the front right side goes over the right shoulder then crosses to the left side of the back and is attached to the front again under the left armpit. The left strap then does the opposite. The designer indicated that some experimentation is needed to get the straps the right length and to get them attached at the right spot so that it fits properly. She indicated that it can be slipped on and off without undoing and retying the straps

Figure 98. *Woman's leather top.*

when it is properly fitted and that this design works well for smaller busted women because this halter provides no support. It is basically a piece of buckskin hanging in front of the bust. Molly also showed that straps can be added to the bottom of the piece and tied together in the back to hold it more securely if desired. Several variations of this design could be used, from a small piece of buckskin, which could double as underwear for a traditional or period dress, to larger pieces that fold around the back and are laced together for more cover. Molly said she came up with the idea for this design because she wanted something cool and light to wear in the heat with her buckskin clothing but did not want to wear a typical bikini bra top. Molly and her family pretty much wear buckskin 365 days a year.

Buckskin Camisole

It has been suggested that a buckskin camisole would be an interesting combination of modern and traditional-type clothing. Old camisoles usually had square necks, and button down fronts. They had either narrow shoulder straps or were strapless with a draw string on top. In making a buckskin camisole cut buckskin wide enough to go from the under arm to the waist, and long enough to go around the bustline. Attach buttons on the front and either shoulder straps or a draw string to the top of the camisole. Fringe or beads could be added for decoration if desired.

Bandeaus or Bandeau Twists

Another interesting suggestion of modern clothing (from the 60's and 70's) to be made from buckskin is a bandeau. A bandeau is a narrow brassiere or strip of cloth wrapped around the bust. Cut a piece of thin buckskin the proper width and long enough to go around the bustline. There are several variations in how a bandeau is worn. It can be just wrapped around and tied either in the back or in front. It can be twisted one half turn in the center front, wrapped around the busts and tied in back. Or, if it is longer, it can be wrapped around from the back of the body, the ends twisted in the center front and then tied behind the neck.

A bandeau could be worn either as outer clothing like a halter top or as underwear with other traditional buckskin clothing.

Other items of buckskin clothing suggested to the author included shorts, panties, crop shirts that lace up the sides, pullover sleeveless shirts that lace up the front, crop jackets, waist jackets and other items.

The author has seen some nice buckskin shorts and tee-shirts made by others. As indicated in the sewing section anything that can be made from fabric can also be made from leather or buckskin. Patterns can be found for almost any item of clothing or a person can modify or make

their own patterns to obtain the desired piece of clothing. Check pattern stores and leather crafting outlets for patterns and ideas.

Sweater with Buckskin

Jesus Montes enrolled in one of my tanning classes a few years ago. He was paired up with another student and together they tanned a deerskin. At the end of the class they split the hide. After some months he called and said that he had a sweater made from his portion of the hide. He told me that his wife had knitted it. She had cut his piece of deerskin in half, made two symmetrical front panels and then knitted the rest of the sweater with a darker buckskin colored yarn. She also covered the buttons with buckskin. This attractive sweater (*Figure 99*) is a good example of combining primitive and modern materials in the same article of clothing.

Buckskin Shirt

This is a great project to make a modern style buckskin shirt; one that is thin enough to wear alone as a shirt in moderate weather or over other clothing like a light jacket in cooler weather. Instead of using a commercial pattern the author chose to take the challenge of trying to make the pattern from an existing shirt. He used a cotton long sleeve shirt from which to create the pattern. See *Figure 100*.

To make the pattern, lay the shirt on newsprint, spread it out and trace around each piece. Weigh the shirt down with books and then trace around each component. If necessary, poke pins in along a seam and then later trace along the holes to mark the pattern. (This was done by the author who is not experienced in making patterns!). If necessary, simplify part of the pattern. Trace the sleeves as a unit and don't attempt to make the cuffs separately. The collar and the front bottom hole piece were simplified in the same manner. The yoke pattern was cut

Figure 99. Sweater with buckskin panels.

Figure 100. Buckskin shirt.

longer than required so that the excess buckskin could be cut into fringe at the back.

After drawing the pattern on newsprint cut the pieces out and find hides that will work for the pattern. It may take a little sorting, picking and trying each pattern piece to decide which hide to use for what piece. It works best to have them match fairly well for thickness, but color is not that important. It took five skins to make this shirt.

Once the hides are picked out, cut the pattern pieces from them. To do this, lay the hides out flat, place the pattern pieces on the hides and weigh them down with books. Then lightly trace around the patterns with a pencil and cut them out. (When doing this pay attention to how the patterns are laid so that either all flesh sides or hair sides come to the outside of the garment.)

Hand sew the shirt together using a needle and flax thread. It works best to use a running stitch, sewing it one direction over and under then coming back over the seam and going over and under in the opposite direction.

Note: Since deer hides come from a round animal they do not always lay perfectly flat after being tanned. The thinner edges are usually somewhat over stretched and will ruffle. These ruffled edges just need to be gathered a little as they are sewed to get the pieces to come out right.

Next, find an antler that is the right diameter and cut cross section pieces for the buttons. Drill small holes in each button and then sew them

Figure 101. Hawk Clinton and Patti Lopez.

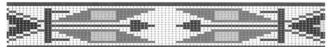

to the shirt. Cut button holes and stitch around them to keep the holes from stretching. Stitch around the edges of the front pieces also to keep them from over stretching.

In *Figure 101*, Hawk Clinton and Patti Lopez are seen modeling their buckskin jacket and shirt. Also, note their buckskin boots (See their sandals and boots on Page 109). Hawk's buckskin jacket is made similar to a capote and has fringe on the shoulders, arms and neck line. It also has a finger woven sash for a belt. Patti is wearing a simple to make yet flattering one-skin blouse made for her by Hawk. She wanted the blouse to be simple, without decoration and the edges left natural. He folded a small deerskin in half, horizontally and then cut a T-shaped hole with pinking shears for the neck along the fold. He then folded the cut edges and stitched them down with buckskin thongs next to the fold to make the neck hole. Then to attach the sides and form sleeves he folded the sides to the back and tied them to the back with two thongs on each side (See *Figure 102*). This type of shirt goes well with primitive or modern attire and for a women is flattering enough to be worn with a modern skirt or pair of pants. With some cre-

ativity this basic pattern could be made into several variations and could, of course, be decorated according to taste.

(See their sandals and boots on Page 109).

One Skin Shirt

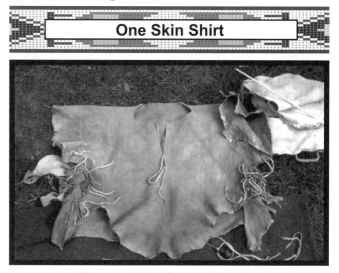

Figure 103. One skin shirt.

Another simple shirt or blouse similar to the one made for Patti that can be made from one skin is shown in *Figure 103*. Trim a hide to a natural symmetrical shape and fold it in half. Cut a neck opening in the center of the fold and add a slit going part way down the chest. Ties can be added to the neck slit if desired. The sides can be attached together with two or three ties on each side. Excess material can be cut into fringe.

Beaver Fur Hat

Several winters ago, David Crockett, a friend of mine, phoned saying he wanted to learn how to brain tan hides. He had trapped two pesky beavers who had been damming off the creek that supplied irrigation water to his ranch. He wanted to make a beaver skin hat. I told him the first steps of brain tanning to get him started. A few days later he called and said "I've got that done what is the next step?" He called a time or two more and I prompted him through the entire brain tanning and smoking process over the telephone. Later, he showed up at my door wearing the beaver skin hat pictured in *Figure 104*. He had done an excellent job of tanning

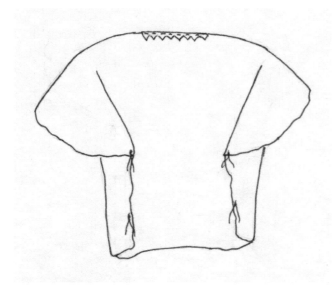

Figure 102. Back view of Patti's shirt.

102

Figure 104. *Beaver fur hat made by Dave Crockett.*

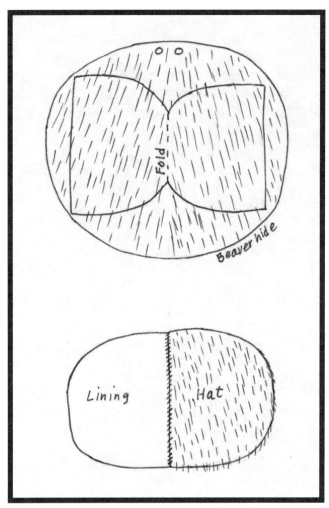

Figure 105. *Beaver fur hat pattern.*

the skin from instructions received over the telephone.

David has a cattle ranch in southern Idaho and is an artist and painter, he does a little hunting and trapping and spends his working hours outdoors. He says he has worn the hat each winter since he made it and that it is warm and durable. The wind can't penetrate it or blow it off and he says it has stood up to rough use when crashing through bushes on his ranch. The hat was several years old when the picture was taken.

MAKING THE HAT

David adapted the following pattern for the hat from a pattern that belongs to his wife. The hat is made from one beaver hide. He wanted the beavers back hair on the top of the hat and the belly hair to be on the bottom of the hat around the ears. So the pattern was laid out as shown in the *Figure 105*. The pattern pieces were oriented so that the front of the beaver was also the front of the hat. In this way the fur laid down from front to back on the hat. It should be noted that this hat can also be made from raccoon, coyote or other fur.

The circumference of the pattern pieces should be about 3 inches more than the head circumference. For example: David's standard hat size is 6 7/8, and his head measurement is about 22 inches around. He cut the pattern pieces so that the circumference of the bottom of the hat was 25 inches. After folding the bottom of the hat up and then back down to make the cuff, it fit just about right. Some experimenting may be necessary to get the right fit. Cut the pieces large and trim if needed.

Lay the pattern out as shown in *Figure 105*. The length of the hat from top to bottom should be sufficient to fold the side up and then back down to form the cuff or band around the ears. The width of the band can be adjusted so that the bottom of the hat comes down over the ears to the desired level.

Cut a lining from a thin material about the same size as the hat pieces. Lay the hat pieces hair sides together. Sew with durable thread, Next sew the lining pieces to the hat, turn the hat right side out and finish sewing the lining together. Fold the side of the hat up to the outside and double the cuff back down to form the cuff or band that goes around the ears. Last pull the lining loose from the band and push it up into the hat. Do not make the lining too small or the hat won't fit down on the head properly.

Vest of Skins

Figure 106.

Joshua Mendenhall, shown in *Figure 106* with his unique vest made from sheepskin and elkskin. He reports it is warm, fun to wear and almost always brings a comment or two from others.

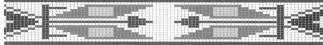

Figure 107. Dave and Marla Bethke.

Pictured above are Dave and Marla Bethke in some of their buckskin clothing. Dave tanned the hides for the pants and the skirt and they were made by Marla. They traded for the shirt and the woman's top at rendezvous. The skirt is a two skin skirt designed and made by Marla. It is made from two skins attached together at the sides and fringed at the seams. It has a few antler buttons on the back at the waist for a closure. Marla does not use patterns but fits the skin to herself and designs the clothing. The top is painted to simulate quillwork. Dave farms in eastern Idaho and brain tans deerskins part time. He was filmed demonstrating how to tan hides as part of a 1990 Idaho Public Television Program titled, "Proceeding on Through a Beautiful Country, a History of Idaho."

Mittens

The mittens shown in *Figure 108* were made by Jim Miller of Mikado Michigan. The palm is made from moose hide and the furry portion is beaver hide. Similar mittens could be made with a buckskin palm and the fur could be from a variety of fur skins.

Figure 109. Mitten pattern.

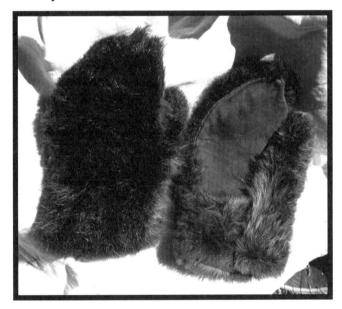

Figure 108. Beaver and moose hide mittens.

The accompanying drawings in *Figure 109* give his basic pattern for the mittens. From these a person can custom make a pattern for their own hand. Some experimentation may be needed to get the pattern to fit properly. Cut only one pattern for each piece as they can be reversed for the other hand. Cut the pieces out of wool blanket scraps or other thick material, sew together and check for fit, then adjust the pattern as needed before cutting buckskin or fur.

Figure 109a - On a piece of paper draw loosely around one hand from wrist to the finger tips. The line should be 1/2 inch or more from the edge of the hand and at least 1/2 inch longer than the fingertips as shown. This is the moose hide piece that will cover the palm of the hand in the mitten.

Figure 109b - Lay the palm pattern on a piece of paper and draw around it enlarging it by about 1/2 to 3/4 inch around the edges. This will be the back part of the mitten made from beaver fur.

Figure 109c - Determine where the bend of the thumb is and mark the pattern as shown. Cut the thumb piece so that it is about 1/2 inch wider and about 1/2 inch longer than the thumb for a seam allowance.

Figure 109d - Draw the rest of the thumb pattern. This piece will be made from the fur. This Pattern piece should be almost 1+1/2 times the width of the other thumb piece and the length will vary depending on how long the cuff will be.

Figure 109e - Draw the cuff the desired width. The piece should be long enough to reach around and attach to each side of the thumb piece. If desired cut it a little short so that the cuff is slightly constricted helping the mitten to stay on the hand better. This piece will be made from the fur.

Figure 109f - Finished mitten.

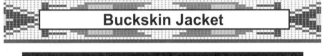

Buckskin Jacket

Figure 110. *Buckskin jacket.*

The buckskin jacket pictured above was made by the French Canadian Indians in the early 1900's and obtained in trade. This jacket is in the collections of the Jerry Lee Young Idaho Heritage Museum, Hollister Idaho. It is a nicely styled jacket and illustrates a good combina-

Figure 111. *Western style buckskin coat.*

tion of modern and primitive styling with fringe and pinking as the only decoration. It has fringe on the front and back and pinking on the cuffs, pockets, shoulders, across the top of the fringe strips and across the bottom of the jacket. The buttons are covered with buckskin and tied to the coat with buckskin strips. The button holes have button hole stitching around them.

Most of the jacket is sewed with a sewing machine but the sleeves and collar are sewed on by hand with a whip stitch.

The coat is made from brain tanned and smoked buckskin of either moose or caribou. The buckskin was wet-scraped and has several patches where the epidermis and grain layer did not come off properly. The jacket was made with the hair side out.

Western Style Buckskin Coat

Buckskin can be made into attractive western wear as shown in *Figure 111*. This buckskin jacket worn by Josh Sage was made by his wife Erin. It has long fringe on the shoulders, short fringe down the side seams and antler buttons.

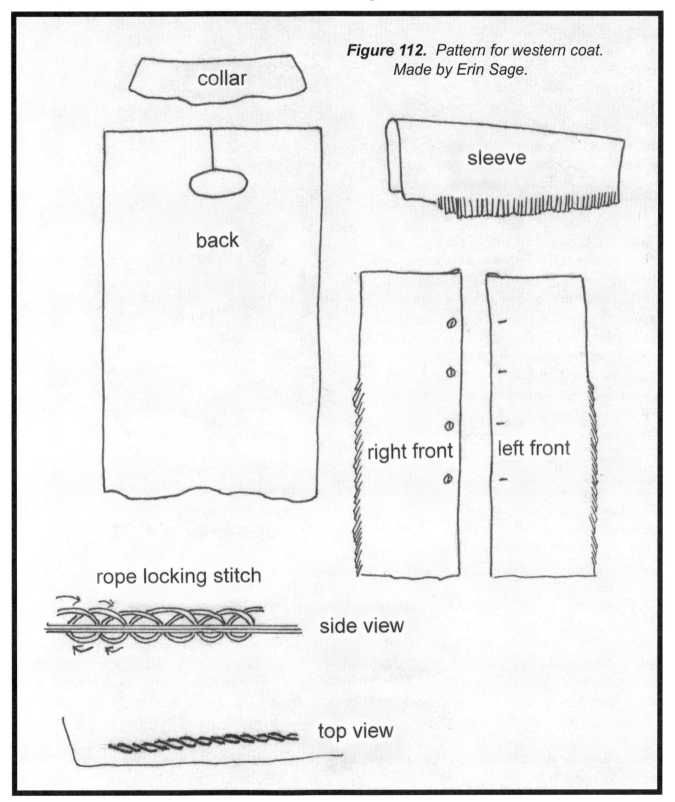

Figure 112. *Pattern for western coat. Made by Erin Sage.*

She made it similar to a western duster but did not use a commercial pattern.

The body of the jacket was made from two large hides. A neck hole was cut in the back hide, as shown in *Figure 112*, and the hide folded over to form the shoulders and the front yoke. The front was formed by splitting a hide down the center, the edges were folded over for buttons and button holes. A hand hole opening was left in each side seam so that the pants pockets can be reached while wearing the coat. The sleeves are pieces of hide folded to fit the arm and sewed together. These were then sewed or laced to the body of the coat. A collar was made from a piece of rough cut buckskin that would reach around the neck. Erin used strips of buckskin to sew all the seams. She used a rope locking stitch at the yoke seam, over the shoulders and to attach the sleeves. Erin explained the rope locking stitch as follows: "The rope locking stitch is a series of loops through the buckskin using each hole twice, once going down from top to bottom and then on the next stitch coming up from bottom to top. It is important to always come up under the last stitch and then to the same side each time in order for it to look like rope on top" (See *Figure 112*).

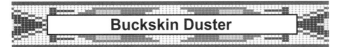

Buckskin Duster

The cowboy duster shown in *Figure 113* is modeled by Neil Gibby. It is made from buckskin using an Eagles View Publishing *Cowboy Duster* Pattern.

For the duster, the skins were brain tanned and smoked and then soaked in a solution of water and ground up black walnut husks to darken them. After soaking, they were allowed to dry, then rinsed and dried again. The hides didn't all retain the color to the same degree, as can be seen in the picture.

The pattern size needed was traced on to news print and some minor modifications were made

Figure 113. Buckskin duster.

to the pattern. The sleeves had two parts but the pattern was traced as one part to avoid any unnecessary seams and sewing. (The whole duster was sewn by hand.) Also the sleeve pattern was curved in a little but was straightened out to make the sleeve a little fuller. The two back pieces were made into one piece, again to avoid extra seams and sewing.

The pattern pieces were taped to the buckskin and weighted down with books before cutting out the buckskin pieces. The pieces were sewn together according to the pattern but the facing pieces were not cut out and sewn. A lining for the coat was made from a surplus wool blanket. Instead of using snaps as suggested in the pattern, buttons from antler were used. Hand

sewing took a lot of time and it would be suggested, if one were to tackle a similar project, to use a sewing machine; unless of course the goal is to do it all by hand!

Foot Wear

The simple and attractive sandal pattern, shown in *Figures 114* and *115*, was developed by Patti Lopez. Patti and Hawk Clinton make much of their own clothing and footwear from brain tanned buckskin and other leather products. This particular pair of sandals was made from commercially tanned leather but they can also be made from buckskin. Patti said that since the pieces are small, the sandals can usually

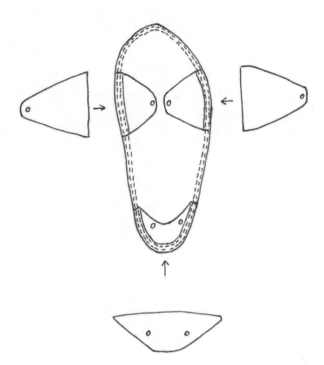

Figure 115. Sandal pattern.

Figure 114. Sandals made by Patti Lopez.

be made from scraps from other projects. She made the sole pattern by tracing around her foot and then drawing another line about 1/4 inch out from the first tracing. She then cut the soles from the leather. For extra padding two leather soles were cut for each foot. The main soles were cut from used rubber conveyer belting that was about 3/8s inch thick. Usually, food manufacturing companies would be a source of the used belting; or, used tires could also be cut into soles.

Patti cut out the front and heel pieces as shown

in the pattern drawings. She indicated that some experimentation may be required to get the pieces the right size and shape. She also indicated that the pieces can be varied for more or less coverage of the foot if desired.

The front pieces do not overlap on top of the foot, but a gap was left so that the sandal can be tightened by the lace. She indicated that the number of lacing holes could be increased if the front pieces were cut wider on top. The heel piece was cut from heavy leather to give the heel support. She stressed that the heel piece should be high enough to not slip off the heel. She also explained that it needs to be cut and attached to the sole in such a way that it slants into the foot a little, making the slipper tight and not away from the foot which would leave the slipper loose and sloppy.

After the pieces were cut, she stitched around them as shown in the Figures. Lacing holes were punched in the pieces in the location shown in the drawings. Next she sewed the pieces to the leather sole with two rows of stitching.

After the leather parts were sewed together, she glued the sandals to the rubber belting soles with a commercial grade water proof contact cement; she advised against using hobby contact cement. Patti said that commercial contact cement can usually be obtained at local shoe repair shops. She coated both pieces with three thick layers of the contact cement, allowing each to dry before adding the next layer. When the layers were dry the pieces were stuck together and pounded with a hammer to be certain all parts were securely glued. She explained that the reason she glues the rubber soles on and does not sew them is so that when the soles wear out they can be peeled off and new ones put on. To do this they heat a pan of water with a piece of foil covering the pan. When the pan is steaming good the shoe is placed on it and heated until the glue starts to melt. Then the sole is grabbed with a pair of vice grips and peeled away from the shoe. Another sole is then glued on.

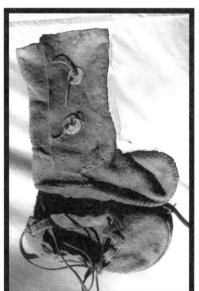

Figure 116. Two piece boots developed by Hawk Clinton.

Patti's husband Hawk developed an interesting concept in buckskin footwear; he makes two piece boots. The inner boot is made similar to a moccasin with a high top and the outer boot is made similar to a moccasin or shoe that is only about ankle high. The outer boot is slipped on and laces tied to hold it to the inner boot. The ob-

jective of the two pieces is so that the outer one can be removed before going into the house and then mud and dirt are not tracked in. The inner boot is worn around the house like a pair of soft moccasins.

To make a pair, find or develop a suitable moccasin pattern that has a high top and a soft buckskin or leather sole. Then make an outer moccasin or shoe similar to the one in the *Figure 116* that will fit over the inner boot. Put either a heavy buckskin sole or a rubber sole on the outer boot as described above. Hawk also makes his own traditional style boots from buckskin (*Figure 117*).

Figure 117. Traditional style boots hand made by Hawk Clinton.

Buckskin Laces

Making buckskin laces for shoes, boots, moccasins and other applications is a simple yet useful project. For shoe or boot laces use a heavy hide, cut the laces a little wider than needed, wet them and stretch them as long as possible. For really tough laces use a hide that has been tanned leaving the epidermis and grain layer. (See the section on tanning while leaving the grain layer.) Allow the laces to dry and apply neatsfoot oil to them or use a mixture of neatsfoot oil with a little beeswax melted into it. If desired, the laces can be dyed dark brown by soaking them in a solution of ground black walnut husks and water. Dry them before applying the oil.

Making laces was once a backwoods industry. Hides were specially tanned with an alum process to produce "lace leather". After tanning and softening, the leather was heavily greased with a mixture of tallow and neatsfoot oil, and then the entire hide was cut into laces.

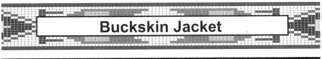

Buckskin Jacket

Figure 118. Major Beeler's jacket.

On October 31, 1864 Mr. James S. Wood a paymaster, wrote a letter to the editor of a paper called the "Missouri Democrat" and recounted the bravery of Major Beeler (the owner of the jacket shown in *Figure 118*) and Major D. C. Smith in saving a steamship (The Belle St. Louis) and its passengers from the attack of some guerrillas.

The guerrillas had rushed on board the boat and had succeeded in forcing the engineers to reverse the engines to return the boat to its landing. The balance of the guerrillas ascended the boats stairs and positioned themselves to guard the entrance to the boats saloon. Major D. C. Smith a Minnesota paymaster and his clerk Mr. A. J. Smith rushed forward to encounter the rebels at the saloon. Major Smith was shot at twice, one bullet missed and the other went through his right arm and entered his body inflicting a mortal wound.

Major Beeler then shot the rebel who killed Major Smith and then ran down the stairs encountering the Lieutenant who was in command of the gang on board. They fired simultaneously, the rebel falling dead, shot through the heart, and Major Beeler receiving the bullet in the breast. The rebels then hearing the shooting suddenly abandoned their posts and jumped into the water for safety, leaving the ship in control of its officers. Major Beeler shortly after his being wounded in this incident recounted the story to Mr. Wood. Mr. Wood in his letter also indicated that all on board had attributed their safety and the safety of the ship to the bravery and intrepidy of Majors Beeler and Smith.

After the Civil War, Major Beeler rode with Buffalo Bill. This jacket later came into the hands of the Whitmore Family and into Tony Whitmores hands who is a great great... nephew of Major Beeler. Tony Whitmore of Hollister Idaho donated the jacket to "Jerry Lee Young's Idaho Heritage Museum" where it is currently housed. The jacket has a patch on the shoulder where Major Beeler was once shot clear through the shoulder with an arrow. Note the fur collar, the buckskin ties at the neck and the leather strip closures that hook over buttons on each side of the jacket. The jacket is lined with material. Decorations include fringe and beading.

The buckskin jacket shown in *Figure 119* is Chippewa/Cree/Metis, circa 1920-1930. The beadwork is very typical of the Turtle Mountain area, with the fringe work and fancy cutting of the cuffs on the sleeves. Also note that there are ties in front not buttons. The jacket was made with the hair side of the skin out. The sleeves and back side of the jacket have heavy scrape marks indicating that the hides were "dry-scraped" brain tanned, and are heavily smoked.

Figure 119. Buckskin jacket from Medora Foundation.

Theodore Roosevelt Medora Foundation, Museum of the Badlands collection.

BAGS, POUCHES, PARFLECHES AND OTHER ITEMS

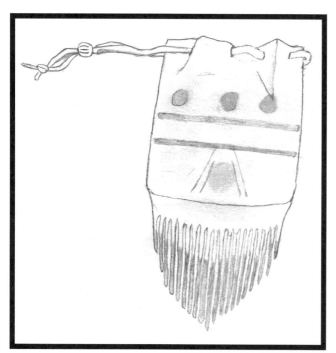

Figure 120. Coin pouch by Blaine Gibby.

In this section, bags, pouches and several other items will be examined and instructions for making most of them are included. Some of these items are traditional and some are modern. Native peoples made many more items from buckskin and rawhide for their daily use than can be included here. By learning the basics of using buckskin and rawhide a person can tackle about any traditional project he or she wishes to try to replicate. Also many modern pieces of clothing and other items can be made from buckskin and rawhide.

Possible Bags

Figure 121 shows a collection of possible bags. The bag on the far left is a day pack made from buckskin and commercial tanned pigskin (See pattern in *Figure 125*, below). The small white

112

Figure 121.

bag and the larger dark bag were both made from felted wool by a friend while he was in Australia.

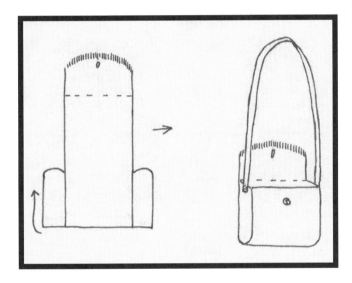

Figure 122. *A basic possible bag pattern.*

The pattern in *Figure 122* shows how to make a basic possibles bag. Other patterns are available and a variety of different styles of possibles bags can be made. The sizes can be adjusted as needed. The main piece and sides can be cut from one piece of hide, but if needed cut the side pieces separately. The bottom can be rounded, as shown, or it can be square. Sew the pieces together, add an antler button closure and cut fringe on the flap if desired. A possible bag can be made as simple or as elaborate as desired.

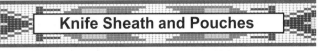

Knife Sheath and Pouches

Figure 123. *Knife sheath and pouches.*

On the knife sheath in *Figure 123*, note that the knife on the left fits completely inside the sheath and has a flap that folds down over the knife. There is also a buckskin thong with a sliding bead to hold the flap closed. In the center is a coin pouch and to the right is a medicine bag with a buckskin thong to go around the neck. All items made by the author.

Medicine bags, small pouches for coins and other items can be made from scraps of buckskin. To make a coin pouch cut a piece of buckskin about six inches by four inches and fold it over flesh side out, place the fringe piece inside and sew the pouch together using a whip or blanket stitch. Turn it right side out, cut the bottom piece into fringe. Then cut a few small slits near the top of the bag and thread a buckskin strip through the slits. Put a bead closure on the strap and tie the end in a knot. The bead should slip a little tight on the strap to close the bag securely. Paint or other decorations can be added as desired.

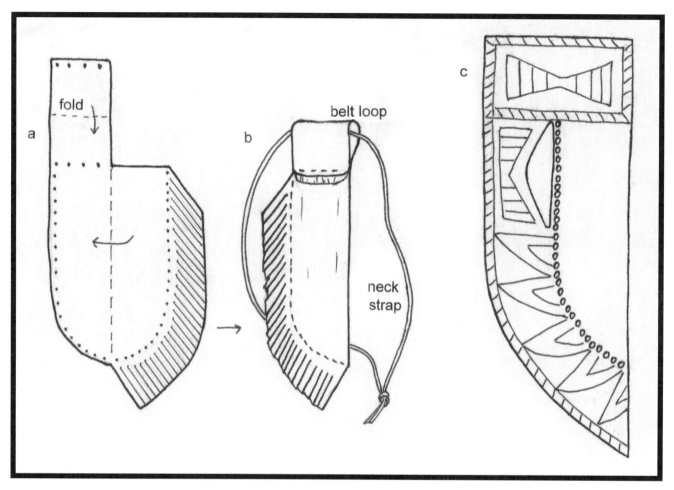

Figure 124. *(a) Pattern for knife sheath shown in* Figure 123. *(b) Finished knife sheath. (c) Standard Blackfoot style knife case, usually made of rawhide and either riveted or laced together. Some were left unadorned, but the standard decorations were beadwork, brass tacks and/ or wool edging. It was worn by putting the belt through the triangular opening.*

Day Pack

Figure 125 is the pattern for the day pack shown in the photograph in *Figure 121*. The day pack is made from pigskin and buckskin. The buckskin has been brain tanned and the pigskin sent to a commercial tannery to be tanned. A number of years ago the author tried to tan some pigskins - it was a complete failure. Someday he will tackle that one again. The idea for this project was to combine the two skins into a day

pack and this is the result. A number of different packs, hand bags, brief cases, etc. could be made from buckskin. Commercial patterns could be obtained for the desired items but no patterns are really needed. It's challenging to try to make up a pattern or trace one from an existing object. Size adjustments can be made and when the object is finished it will be custom made to personal needs.

For the day pack shown in *Figure 125*, a pattern was made by combining ideas from two commercial day packs commonly used by kids for school. The drawing shows the sizes used for each piece and how the parts are put together. The size can be varied to personal taste. If a large enough hide is available the front, back, top, bottom and sides can all be cut out in one piece and less sewing is required to put it together. Otherwise the pieces can be cut from smaller hides and more seams will be needed

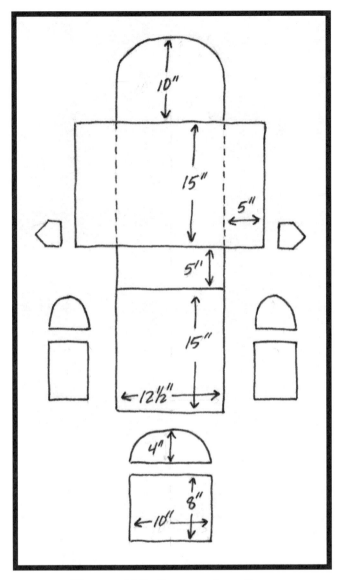

Figure 125. Day pack pattern.

gusset at the bottom of the pack and a piece of hide sewed over the straps at the top, as shown. Straps and plastic quick release attachments were added for a closure.

Concealed Purse

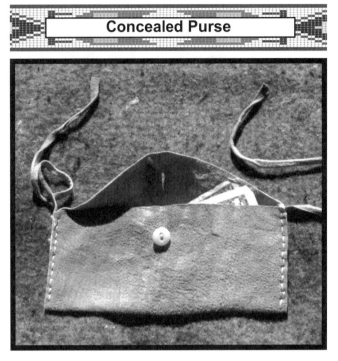

Figure 126. Woman's concealed purse.

The handy concealed purse illustrated in *Figure 126* can be worn under a woman's clothing attached to her bra. The two tie straps on the purse are used to tie it to the bra straps. To make one, cut a piece of thin buckskin approximately 9 inches x 7 inches. Fold the buckskin, leaving two inches for a closure flap and sew together. Sew a narrow buckskin strap, six or eight inches long, to each side of the purse. The two inch flap is cut like an envelope flap, a button hole put in it and a button is attached to the front of the purse.

The author made one for his wife for a cross country trip to a large city. At her return she said she had carried her currency with confidence!

to sew the back pack together. Sew the back pocket and flap on before sewing the main pieces together. Side pockets can be added, as shown, but are optional.

A seam allowance of about 1/4 inch was used on all pieces. An awl was used to punch holes and it was sewn all by hand; a sewing machine could also be used if desired. It was sewn with artificial sinew and a running stitch was used.

The straps were purchased from a surplus store and fittings were added so that they could be adjusted. The straps were attached using a

Parfleche

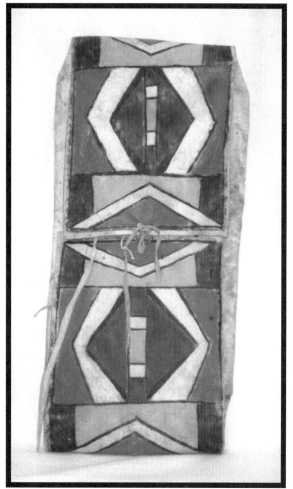

Figure 127. Parfleche, probably cowhide, decorated in red, blue, green and yellow. From the Native American Collection, Gordon B. Olson Library, Minot State University, Minot, North Dakota. Photographed by Harold Aleshire.

The word parfleche (pronounced par'-flesh) comes from the French, meaning "to parry arrows". Early French men first seeing them, thought they were shields.

A parfleche is a rawhide container and was usually made by the Indian women of the Plains. They were made in various sizes and designs but were usually shaped somewhat like an envelope. In early times, they were loaded with dried buffalo strips, pemmican or other food for storage. They were also used to store household utensils, clothing and other items. A buffalo hide was sometimes made into two large parfleches for storing clothing. A well furnished teepee usually included numerous parfleches.

When traveling or moving, the women would tie the parfleches to their dogs and they were used as packs. Later when horses were introduced by the whites they were used as packs on the horses.

Women worked the rawhide including making parfleches. The hides were cleaned and scraped and geometric designs were painted on the hide using bones as brushes and vegetable or mineral colors as paint. The parfleche was then cut out and softened by repeated pounding of the rawhide. Holes were burned in for tie straps and buckskin laces were added.

Women gained prestige and profit from well made and well decorated parfleches. In later years, the parfleches were used more for decoration than for practical use. They were cherished as mementos of the buffalo days. They were always appropriate as gifts and often the fate of a gift parfleche was to be cut up into moccasin soles.

Making a Parfleche

Many of the techniques and terms in this segment are explained in detail in Section III.

Step 1. If the hide is dry, soak it a day or two in water until soft, then thoroughly flesh the hide.

Step 2. The hide is then soaked again for a few days to allow the hair to slip. The addition of some wood ashes to the solution helps to slip the hair; change the water daily to help keep the odor down.

Step 3. Scrape the hair off the hide. It is not necessary to scrape the grain layer from the hide

begins to dry, dampen it by blotting water on it. Use hot water in the paint to help it soak into the hide. Another method is to coat the painted area with hide glue to help seal the paint into the hide. Allow the hide to dry. (Some Natives would paint the designs on the hide before the hair was removed, then scrape the hair off later.) Paints were from animal, vegetable, and mineral sources; mineral paints were most common. Native women painted geometric designs on parfleches with porous buffalo bones.

Step 6. Cut the parfleche from the hide and burn or punch holes in the edges according to the accompanying drawing in *Figure 128.*

Step 7. The last step is to soften the parfleche. Natives did this by laying the hide on a pad of blankets or old hides and pounding it with a smooth rock until it was soft and creamy white. This is almost an unbearably long and tedious project. It is preferred to fold and bend the hide in numerous places and roll it back and forth on itself until it is reasonably soft. The hide can also be worked across a sharp edge and softened. Some say that if the grain layer is scraped off, the hide will soften up with pounding. Lac-

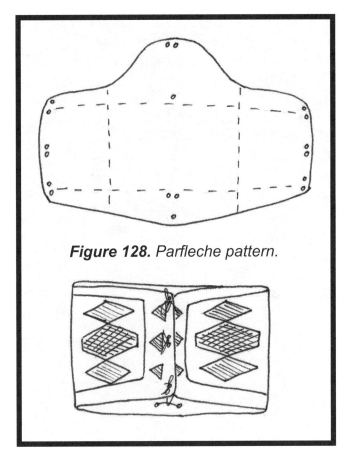

Figure 128. *Parfleche pattern.*

but some suggest that it is easier to soften the hide if the grain layer is removed.

An alternative to #2 and #3, above, is to stretch the hide in a stretching frame after fleshing. Then after it dries, scrape the hair and grain layer from the hide with a dry scrape tool in the same manner as when preparing it for brain tanning.

Step 4. Stretch the hide in a frame or stake out tight on the ground, flesh side up.

Step 5. Draw the parfleche shape on the flesh side of the hide and paint the design areas while the hide is still damp. If the hide

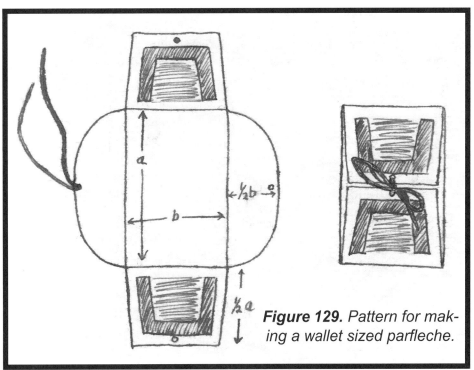

Figure 129. *Pattern for making a wallet sized parfleche.*

ing thongs can now be added and the parfleche folded as shown. It is ready for use.

Period Wallet

An authentic period wallet can be made by making a small parfleche. To make the pattern draw a rectangle about 3 1/2 inches by 5 inches, then make each end flap one half the length and each side flap one half the width of the original rectangle as shown in the drawing on Page 117 in *Figuer 129*. Cut the parfleche from rawhide, soften as described above and decorate to taste. Only one hole needs to be punched in the end of each flap as shown. Put in a leather tie and the project is complete, except for putting in a few greenbacks!

TIPS FOR SEWING BUCKSKIN

One of the most important things to do with buckskin before making any clothing is to wet or wash it and let it dry a time or two. This important step is often overlooked, but it will help the skin to return to its natural shape and size before the clothing is made. Otherwise when the clothing does get wet, or washed, it may dry into a much different shape than it was when made. To do this, wet the skin and if desired wash it in mild soap, rinse and then gently squeeze the water out, don't wring it or it will be stretched out of shape again. Then lay the skin out flat on a towel or blanket and allow to dry without further stretching or working. When it is dry just fluff or rub it together a few times to re-soften it.

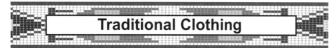

Traditional Clothing

Don't plan clothing before the hides are tanned! Hides don't always come out how a person thinks they will. The thickness and softness may not be what was expected and hides always seem to be smaller after they are tanned. It is better to tan several hides and then pick the ones that will best suit the clothing that is planned. However some generalizations can be made. Big thick hides can be planned for heavy outer clothing, moccasins, belts, knife sheaths and bags. Thinner hides may be more suitable for light clothing such as shirts, blouses, skirts, underwear, children's clothing or for small pouches etc.

When making traditional clothing without patterns, make everything loose and big. Put seams or ties in an inch or more from the edge of the piece and cut the excess into fringe.

traditional clothing is often tied together with strips of buckskin. Punch holes in the edges of the two pieces and tie with strips of buckskin. A second method is to use buckskin strips with either one or two holes punched near one end of the lace. When the lace is put through the clothing, it is laced back through the holes to hold it in place. These laces are easily loosened or removed to loosen clothing in warm weather.

If sewing with buckskin thongs, cut them from the flesh side of the skin to see and avoid scores and other weak areas. Cut the lace a little wider than needed then wet it and stretch it as long as possible so that it will not stretch in the clothing with use. If a piece of buckskin is cut in a spiral it can be made into one long strand of lace.

Buckskin is quite stretchy, especially when wet, and to keep edges of clothing, necklines etc. from stretching out of shape fold the edges of the skin over and sew it in a running stitch with thread or a buckskin lace. One young woman at a rendezvous told how she had made a buckskin top and was wearing it in a canoe when it capsized spilling her into the water. She said her blouse was completely drenched and when she emerged from the water it was with an "ever expanding neckline!" After that she began putting running stitches into the edges of her buckskin clothing.

Tailoring a Neckline

The neck hole on a piece of clothing should always be shifted a short distance forward of the center line of the shoulders for the garment to hang properly. In making binary shirts or dresses (See *Figure 78*) make the back shoulder and neck lines a little higher than the front neck and shoulder lines. The front neck line will scoop down lower in the material than the back one. Attach them together at the armpit and sides first, then fold the back piece down to sew to front piece.

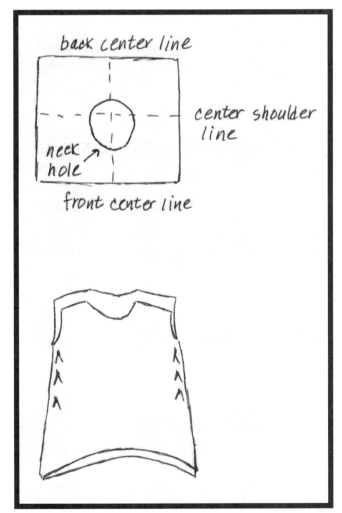

Figure 130. *How to shift the neck hole forward for proper tailoring.*

When cutting a neck hole into a poncho type top, the neck hole should be shifted forward of the shoulder line a short distance. If the neck hole is just centered at the shoulder line the back of the neck will tend to hang down and the front of the neck will tend to ride up.

Modern Clothing

Modern style clothing can be made from buckskin using standard fabric patterns and sewing by hand or using a regular home sewing machine. Make modern clothing from buckskin a bit larger and looser than fabric clothing because buckskin is usually a little heavier. Tandy Leather Company has at least two good references for making clothing from leather on a home sewing machine. They have a video titled "Sewing with Leather" and a booklet also with the same title. The principles would also apply to making clothing from buckskin. The following few tips from these two sources should get a person started if they desire to sew buckskin on a home sewing machine. For more details one should consult these and other sources.

1 - Anything that can be made from fabric can also be made from buckskin.

2 - If the pattern says to cut on fold, instead make the other half of the pattern and tape the two pieces together. Then lay the hide out flat, tape the pattern to it and then cut out the pieces.

3 - Use leather needles (Glover's needles with a triangular point) on the machine and set the stitch length somewhere between seven and ten stitches per inch.

4 - When seams are sewn, fold the seam allowance down flat and glue with rubber cement. (Some experimentation would be needed to test this with buckskin). To finish edges, fold seam allowance over and top stitch it down.

5 - Modern style skirts and jackets should be lined, so they will hang and drape better. The linings can be stitched in by hand if desired. A half slip makes a good skirt lining as it can be stitched to the waist band or just worn under the skirt.

Laying Out Pattern Pieces

Keep in mind when laying out pattern pieces that deer and humans are both bilaterally symmetrical. This means that from the back bone, the right side of the body is a mirror image of the left side. The skin has equal stretch on either side of the backbone. When laying out patterns align the pieces so that the length of the garment will line up with the backbone of the hide. For example, fronts and backs of shirts blouses etc. and long sleeves. When the clothing is worn, the length of the hides backbone will be parallel with the persons backbone or the backbone of the hide will run down the center of the sleeve. Patterns for pieces that fit the body left to right such as yokes and collars can be placed on the hide crosswise, or left to right, with the center of the pattern aligned with the hides backbone. Smaller left and right pieces of clothing (such as cuffs, pockets, mittens etc.) can be placed as mirror images of each other, equidistant on each side of the backbone of the hide. Avoid placing pattern parts on an angle or bias of the backbone line. If these principles are followed, clothing should hang better and stretch and shrinkage will be more uniform.

Stitches

In *Figure 131*, the following stitches are illustrated:

(a) Top stitch or running stitch. This is used for attaching bands and borders; for reinforcement or for decoration when contrasting colors of thread are used. It can be used as a baste stitch to temporarily attach pieces together and removed after a more secure stitch is sewn.

(b) Running stitch. Same as above but come back in the opposite direction for a more secure stitch. Some people use two needles and do both seams at once. The author prefers this stitch for seams and edges. Fold the edge of the buckskin over and sew in this manner to give it a finished edge.

(c) Whip stitch. Used for seams and moccasins.

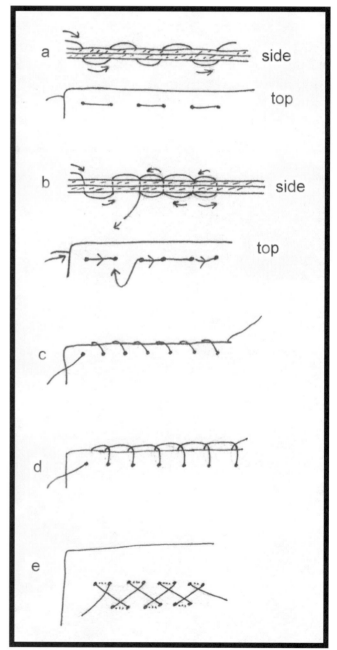

Figure 131. *Illustration of various stitches.*

120

(d) Blanket stitch or button hole stitch. Use to finish a cut edge or for seams. Also good for decoration when using contrasting colors.

(e) Mending stitch. Used for mending or repairs to buckskin.

CLEANING BUCKSKIN

Care and Cleaning

Buckskins can be washed by hand or by machine. Hand washing is accomplished by simply using a mild soap and cool or lukewarm water and doing it by hand. (Ivory Soap® is recommended for cleaning leather by it's makers). Sometimes a stiff brush or pumice stone is needed to remove stubborn stains. Smoked skins will lighten with time as they are washed. Therefore, some people who wear skins a greater part of the year like to dye their buckskins to help retain the color longer. (See section on dyeing skins.)

Machine Wash

If needed scrub dirty spots with a brush and soap before washing. Use warm water (not hot enough to burn hands) and the delicate or gentle cycle. Use soft mild soap.

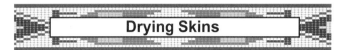

Drying Skins

The best way to dry buckskin clothing is to gently squeeze not wring the water from the clothing, lay the item down on a towel or blanket, try to form it to the proper shape and let it dry. After it dries just ruffle it a little to restore its softness. Wearing the clothing will also restore its softness.

Machine Drying

Use cool cycle and watch the skins closely, take them out frequently and ruffle up and check dryness. Take out when still damp and put on, as the clothing dries it will form to the body. If the clothing can't be put on, hang it or lay it down on a blanket or towel and try to form it to the proper shape. The skin will dry a little stiff but will soften up easily as it is worn or if it is ruffled up in the hands a little.

NOTES

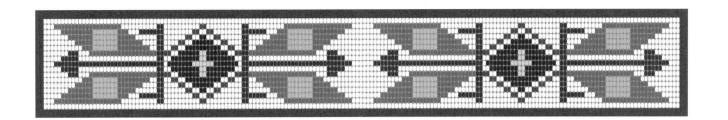

SECTION III

TANNING BUCKSKIN
AND FUR

Brain tanning is not an exact science. It is an art. It is like cooking. If several people are given the same recipe and asked to cook it, the resulting dishes would not be identical but each would vary to some degree. So it is with brain tanning. It is the author's opinion that each person's interpretation and application of the instructions affect the way their buckskins turn out. And, while different people's buckskins do not turn out identical when using the same basic techniques, each hide can be just as effec-

tively tanned, but varying in some esthetic quality.

A practical approach to brain tanning then would be to try several techniques and procedures, gain experience in tanning and let the hides develop their personalities as a result. After one finds results they like, then concentrate on perfecting those particular techniques that produce the desired results and qualities.

BUCKSKIN TANNING - TANNING WITH THE HAIR OFF

Tanning processes similar to those described in this section were used by most of the pre-contact Native groups in America. Tanning was done primarily by the Indian women who were the worlds "masters" at processing animal skins into usable buckskins and furs. Their buckskins were much stronger than cloth yet with their methods the hides were made as soft and supple as the softest cloth. They were able to do this using a minimum of tools, all made from natural materials found in their environment. The tanned hides were made into tipis, buckskin clothing, robes, bags and other useful items. A family's buckskins could get wet many times and still dry as soft as ever because of the women's expertise in properly processing the skins.

The methods described in this section produce skins that are, in essence, the same as buckskins and furs tanned by the Native Americans. Using a few homemade tools (described in the tools for tanning section) and these techniques anyone can produce skins of excellent quality. These methods are straightforward and no more difficult than tanning with a modern kit.

history by American Indians to process animal skins into usable material. Some early settlers regarded buckskin made by Indians and others as a makeshift product and not real leather. It was considered inferior to modern tanned leather. But this is not true; buckskin properly made the Indian way is durable, light and soft as flannel. Brain tanning is an ideal method for home tanners since the only tanning agent needed is animal brains. No acids or hazardous tanning solutions are required. The tools and equipment needed are easily homemade or inexpensively acquired.

A number of brain tanning methods have been described by early explorers among the Indians. Each Indian tribe or group seemed to have their own particular methods but the processes and the end product are basically about the same. Brain tanning is the process of mechanically separating the fibers of the hide, lubricating them with oils from the brain tissue and giving the hide the ability to dry soft by the application of smoke.

Native buckskin making included at least the following basic steps. Again with different groups or individuals having variations in the way these steps were accomplished:

The Brain Tanning Method

Brain tanning was developed before recorded

1. Removal of fat, flesh and membrane from the

skin. The fat and flesh were basically just scraped off with bone or stone tools. The skin was pegged out flat on the ground or it was laid over a log leaned up to a tree.

2. Removal of the hair and grain layer from the skin. Hair and grain layer was sometimes scraped off while the skin was wet; today called wet-scrape brain tanning (See notes at end of this section for a brief description of wet-scrape brain tanning). Or, the skin could be stretched out in a frame or on the ground and allowed to dry. Then the hair and grain layer was scraped off with sharp stone tools; today called dry-scrape brain tanning. Skins sometimes were also soaked in ashes and water until the hair slipped and could be easily scraped off. The grain layer includes the epidermis. (See Deerskin Structure and Makeup section.)

3. Braining the skin. The skin was either soaked in a brain solution or the brains were made into a paste and rubbed directly onto the skin. This process also involved some kind of skin manipulation to thoroughly work the brains into the skin. Other materials were sometimes used with the brains such as spinal cord, liver, marrow, fat and vegetable matter, but brains seemed to be the one main ingredient.

4. Breaking (softening) and drying the skin. This step involved stretching and working the skin in some manner until it was completely dry and soft.

5. Smoking the skin. This step may not have been universally practiced, but by smoking the skins they could be softened easier after washing or getting wet and insects would no longer bother them. Smoking was accomplished in several ways: The skin was hung over a slow smoky fire to absorb smoke. The fire could be built in a hole in the ground and the skin hung over it in the form of a bag or it could be draped over a framework of sticks. Sometimes the skins were hung up in the smoke holes of their lodges or placed in special small smoke houses. Sometimes skins were dyed, painted or decorated in some manner, but this was not an essential step.

DRY-SCRAPE BRAIN TANNING

This section describes how to make genuine buckskin in much the same way that native Americans made it even before the settlement of North America by the whites (See Wet-Scrape Brain Tanning section for a comparison with this technique). In this method, the hair and grain layer will be scraped off the skin while dry and when properly tanned, the skin will be as soft as flannel. This method may be used for deer, elk, antelope, goat, or other skins. It may be preferable to begin with a small skin.

Preparing the skin. Try to get a fresh unsalted skin, but if it has been salted or dried, soak and rinse the skin well to soften it and to remove the salt. It is a good idea to soak a skin overnight in water even if it is fresh as this will help to loosen dirt, wash out blood and wet any edges that may have begun to dry. After the soak, rinse the skin well and hang it up to allow it to drip.

Fleshing Skins

The skin can be laid over a smooth log that is leaned up against a tree or shed as shown in *Figure 132*. The skin should be at a comfortable working height. Straddle the skin and with the fleshing tool, held in both hands, begin pulling it down into the flesh removing it from the skin. As the flesh is pulled off, move the skin around on the beam to expose other areas on which to work.

Another method to flesh a hide is to do it over a beam that is mounted on legs and slants from about waist height to the ground (See *Tools for Tanning* section for instructions for making fleshing tools and a fleshing beam). To use this tool, drape the hide over the beam and allow the edge to fall off the top end a little. Lean against this edge to secure the hide and with the fleshing tool begin pushing the flesh off the hide. Again, move the hide around to get all parts of it fleshed. Keep the area of the hide that is being worked at the top of the beam.

Hold the fleshing tool so that the flat edge is down and the beveled edge is pushed or pulled into the flesh at an angle so that it digs in and removes the flesh. The cutting edge of the fleshing tool should be slightly dulled so that it will not cut the hide. Sometimes pieces of flesh can be cut or pulled off by hand.

Figure 132. Fleshing the skin. Note, the skin is being fleshed with a deer bone; the front leg bone containing the ulna and radius.

Scrape off all of the meat, fat and membrane. The meat and fat are fairly obvious to identify and should all be removed. The membrane is a thin mostly cloudy or clear layer that often adheres to the skin even after the fat and flesh are removed. Scrape this off as much as possible. If any membrane is left on and dries it can be pulled off in sheets or dry-scraped off

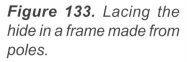

Figure 133. Lacing the hide in a frame made from poles.

Figure 134. Hide pegged and stretched on the ground.

later. Next, if desired, trim the rough edges and the ends of the legs, etc. so the skin has a nice symmetrical shape. After some experience with tanning one can try tanning the entire skin without trimming the legs, tail or rough edges. Some articles of traditional clothing are more authentic when made with complete deerskins.

Stretching the Hide in a Frame

With a sharp knife point, make inch long cuts about a half inch from the edge of the skin and about 5" to 6" apart all around the edge. These cuts should be parallel to the edge of the skin. Build a stretching frame from 2x4's or small poles as shown in *Figure 133*. These can be nailed, bolted or lashed, but be sure to build a solid frame so that, as the skin dries and shrinks, it will not twist the frame or pull it apart. Lay the frame down on the ground and lay the skin in the frame, flesh side up with the neck to the top of the frame. Lace the skin into the frame with baling twine or similar cord.

Use four lengths of twine: one on each side of the frame. Carefully tighten each string until the skin is stretched out flat but not over stretched. Try to keep the skin in it's natural

shape by not pulling it too long, too wide or skewed at an angle. The skin should now be allowed to dry. Keep it inside a building if there is threat of storms or rain. As shown in *Figure 134*, sometimes hides would be pegged and stretched on the ground, to be fleshed and dehaired, when poles were not available for stretching frames.

Removing the Hair and Grain Layer

After the skin is completely dry, the hair and grain layer can be scraped off; see the *Tools for Tanning* section for instructions for making a hide scraper. Hold the scraping tool so that the blade is at a right angle or less to the skin. If the blade is held at too sharp of an angle it may dig into and cut the skin.

Start at the neck of the hide and begin scraping at the hair until a small patch is removed and the bare hide is visible underneath. Then begin carefully scraping at the bare hide until the blade is cutting small curls of hair and the attached grain layer from the skin. Gradually enlarge the bare spot and begin scraping in a pattern across the skin. Each scraping stroke should be taken in the general direction from neck to tail or at a

Figure 135. Scraping the hair from the dried skin.

slight angle from neck to tail. This is the direction that the hair lays. Take short even strokes moving in a systematic pattern across the hide, clearing a two or three inch wide strip each time across.

One of the most important things to remember in dry scraping is to not get in a hurry and to try to take long sweeping strokes. The author has seen more hides ripped from long careless strokes than for any other reason. The blade should only contact the hide and scrape off material on the downward pull, lift the tool away from the hide on the up swing. On each downward stroke begin cutting into the hide slightly above the hair in a place that has already been scraped. Keep the tool sharp, with each stroke it should be shaving off small curls of skin (grain

layer) with hair attached.

Don't try to cut too deeply with each stroke. Instead, if needed, go over the same area several times until all the hair and the grain layer are removed. The grain layer should be completely removed in order for the skin to properly tan flannel soft. The hide should have a white or creamy white color and sometimes fuzzy look to it when it is properly scraped. If the hide has patches of visible hair roots or is quite gray it should be scraped more.

If most or all of the hair roots (stubble) are removed the hide will be sufficiently scraped. It is possible that a hide will turn out fine even when some hair roots are still attached. If it seems difficult to get all the hair roots out, the hide can be wet scraped later, while it is being brained, to clean up any remaining grain and roots.

This method takes a little practice, but experimenting with it a little will soon help perfect the technique. Scraping is rather tedious work, but if done correctly the quality of the finished product justifies the effort. Again, don't worry about removing the hair from the edges of the skin, but be careful not to tear the skin.

Figure 136. Dried and scraped skins rolled for storage. Two of the skins were wet scraped and just laid over a pole to dry, so they were not rolled up.

128

While dry scraping watch for bullet holes and knife cuts and work around these carefully so as to not rip them out larger. It helps to poke little sticks through the holes from the flesh side to make them visible from the hair side. Also scrape the belly and flanks carefully since they are thin and can tear easily. The rump skin can also tear easily, it is thicker than the belly and flanks but seems to be softer and is sometimes waxy or greasy making it more difficult to scrape.

After the hair and grain layer are removed, check the flesh side of the skin for any remaining membrane. For best results in the finished skin, it is important to completely remove any remaining membrane from the flesh side of the skin. This can be done by dry scraping the same way that the hair and grain layer was removed. Finish by sanding both sides of the skin lightly with coarse sand paper or a pumice stone.

Carefully cut the skin out of the frame by cutting about 1/2" from the edge, leaving the un-scraped outside edge of skin and holes in the frame. If desired, wash the skin for a few minutes in warm soapy water to remove any remaining soil, blood and fat, then rinse the skin and wring it out well. The skin is now ready to be brain tanned. If there is not enough time to tan the skin at this point, remove the dry skin from the frame, trim the edges, roll the skin into a tube and store it as shown in *Figure 136*.

Figure 137. One method of braining the skin is to soak it in a solution of water and brains.

Braining the Skin – Method One

For one average size deerskin use the equivalent of about one deer brain or use the brain from the deer that the skin came from if it is available. Otherwise, use about 1-2 cups of cattle or pork brains (available from butcher shops and grocery stores). Add a small amount of warm water to the brains and mash them to a fine, pasty consistency or pulverize the brains in a home blender. Add this solution to 1 or 2 gallons of warm water in a bucket and mix well. The brain solution should be boiled for several

minutes to kill bacteria before adding it to the bucket of water. Be certain that the brain and water solution is not too hot to the touch before putting the hide in it as described in the next step.

Thoroughly dampen the skin in warm water and then submerge it in the brain solution. Agitate the skin and get all parts wet. It is important that all parts of the skin be saturated with the solution. As the skin becomes saturated, it will become very limp and flexible. The next step is to wring the skin out well. It can be done by wringing it around a rope tied vertically from the base of a tree and then to a branch about head high. Or the hide can be wrung around a horizontally mounted pole about waist high. Remove the hide from the solution and squeeze it over the bucket. Flatten the skin out and wrap

Figure 138. Wringing the brains from the skin.

oil from the brains as possible. The properly saturated and wrung skin will be milky white and very stretchy. If it is only just wet, the skin will not be stretchy and will have the appearance of wet paper. The purpose of the soaking and wringing process is to stretch the skin, separate the fibers and allow complete penetration (or saturation) of the brain solution into the fibers. In order to promote good fiber separation and penetration of the brain solution, More time should be spent wringing the skin than sloshing the skin in the solution. The skin can be sloshed around in the solution for a few seconds then several minutes are required to give it a thorough wringing. At the last wringing twist the skin tight from several angles to get as much liquid out as possible. An old towel can be wrapped around the skin to further absorb moisture.

A variation of the above braining process is to soak and wring the skin several times in the brain solution and then let it soak overnight. The following morning it can be wrung and submerged a few more times and then be taken to the next step.

it into a tube around the rope or pole over-lapping about 1/3 of the width of the skin.

Now roll the skin into a donut around the rope or pole. Insert a stick and twist the skin very tightly to wring out the brain solution. Untwist the stick, rotate the donut 90 degrees, and twist again. Unroll the skin, submerge it again in the brain solution, and agitate it for a few minutes. Remove the skin from the bucket and repeat the wringing process with the rope or pole and stick. This submerging and wringing process should be repeated 5-6 times for light skins and up to 8-12 times for heavy skins, or as many times as it takes to get the skin completely saturated. At the end of the process all parts of the skin should be thoroughly saturated with the brain solution and will have taken up as much

Note: During the braining process, if it appears that there may be some grain or hair roots still attached, put the hide over the beam and wet scrape it with the fleshing tool. Use the same scraping process that was used for fleshing. This will not only help to remove the remaining grain and hair roots but will also help to stretch and separate the fibers and allow better brain penetration. After wet scraping go back to the braining and wringing process as above.

Braining the Skin – Method Two

Mix about a pound of brains (depending on the size of the hide) with about half its volume of water and mash the mixture to a thin pasty consistency. Or, better yet, mix it in a home blender. Heat the mixture to about 100 degrees F, but not too hot to the touch. Work the brain mixture into both sides of the hide with a smooth, flat stone. Continue working the mixture in until both sides of the skin are completely saturated with the brains.

After working the brains in, roll the skin up and place it in a plastic bag for a few hours or overnight to assure complete saturation of the skin with the brains. When the skin is removed from the bag, scrape off any excess brain tissue and wring the skin out well.

After either method of braining the skin, take some artificial sinew or other strong thread and sew up any bullet holes or cuts found in the skin. This is best done while the skin is wet and pliable. Wax the thread and use a whip stitch sewing from the flesh side of the hide. Leave the ends of the thread about two inches long and trim them after the breaking and drying process.

Breaking and Drying Skins

Figure 139. *Breaking (softening) and drying the skin.*

The next step is breaking and drying the skin. To accomplish this step, the skin must be pulled and stretched until it is completely dry and soft. After the skin has been removed from the brain solution and wrung out well, it can be hung up for a short time to begin to dry, but be careful not to allow the skin to stand long enough for any area to harden. Place the skin behind the rope used for wringing, grab it on both sides of the rope, and pull firmly. Move the hands further from the rope and pull again. Finally, move to the edge of the skin and pull and stretch. Move the hide at different angles and repeat this process. While stretching the hide, periodically pull it vigorously back and forth across the rope to help fluff it up. At first, while the hide is quite wet mostly stretch it, but as it begins to dry, then it can be see-sawed across the rope more often. This stretching and see-sawing should be done mostly on the grain side of the hide. Work the edges of the hide over the rope once in awhile to get them soft.

Continue this process at intervals until the skin turns milky white and is soft and dry. It is important to keep the fibers in the hide moving until the hide is dry so that it will be soft. The more it is stretched and worked at this time, the softer the buckskin will be. It is fine to take short breaks but don't leave the hide long enough for it to dry and stiffen up. The breaking and drying process may take several hours so plan a day when there is plenty of time to devote to it. If a person gets part way through the breaking process and must stop before it is completed, just wrap the hide up in a damp towel, place in a plastic bag and store it overnight in a cool place.

Generally the hardest parts of the hide to soften, and the last parts to dry, are the neck and the rump. When the hide gets to the point where it seems like the neck and rump are never going to dry, but are beginning to stiffen a little, double the effort and work those specific areas twice as hard over the rope. Put the pull to it and see-saw it back and forth with heavy and rapid strokes in all directions. The faster sawing generates heat and speeds up drying and the harder pulling stretches and works the hide deeper. This almost always gets those spots dry and soft.

Skins can be broken over a metal strap instead of a rope. This was demonstrated by Randy Breeuwsma, from Alberta, Canada to a group at a Rabbitstick Rendezvous in Idaho. He used a piece of strap iron about 1 1/2 or 2 inches wide and 1/8 inch thick. It was bent into an arc and both ends securely fastened to a tree. When breaking a skin he would pull it and work across the metal in the same manner as described above for the rope.

Another breaking method used frequently is called staking (See the section on *Tools for Tanning* for instructions to make a staking tool). The skin is worked and stretched over it in a manner similar to shining shoes until it is dry and soft.

A method similar to this called frame staking was used by the Indians. The skin was either tanned while stretched in the frame, or was tanned and laced back into the frame to be broken and dried. For best results, allow the lacing to be a little loose. This method also can be used for deer skins with the hair left on.

To use this method, get a two inch diameter pole about four feet long. Round one end and flatten the other into a rounded edge (See Tools for Tanning section). Stand the frame and hide up against a shed or something solid. Push the pole into and stretch all areas of the hide. Next, scrape and stretch all over the hide with the flattened end to further break the hide. Don't be afraid to apply some pressure, but do it with care. The more the skin is worked, the softer it will be.

This scraping and stretching should be continued until the skin is dry and soft. If dealing with

a heavy skin that is difficult to soften, leave it laced into the frame, rub brains into both sides again and work the skin dry a second time. Remove it from the frame and trim off any rough or hard edges.

Smoking Skins

The American Indians smoked their buckskins to give them the ability to dry soft after getting wet. Smoking also colors the skin and protects it from insect pests. This is an important step, not to be overlooked in brain tanning.

The usual smoking material is punky (rotted) wood, but wood chips, bark, grass, leaves or any material that can be burned and produce smoke can be used. Fallen rotted logs from forested areas are good sources of punky wood. Usually large quantities of soft broken up material can be gathered. It is easy to see that in these areas the Natives had an abundant sup-

Figure 140. *Smoking a deerskin.*

132

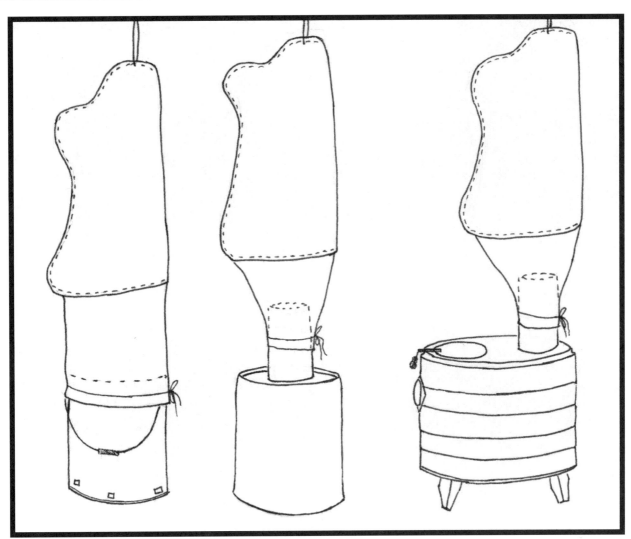

Figure 141. *Different methods of smoking skins.*

ply of material for smoking their buckskins.

Smoking a skin can be accomplished in several ways. Cool smoke is needed so that the heat does not damage the skins. If only one skin is to be smoked, fold it along the backbone and sew it from the neck to the hind leg forming it into a bag. Then sew a two or three foot long canvas sleeve to the bottom or opening. Two hides can also be smoked this way by sewing then together forming a bag and adding the sleeve in the same manner. Punch a few half inch diameter air holes in the side at the bottom of a five gallon metal bucket. Start a fire in the bucket and let it burn down to coals. Add the punky wood or other material to produce smoke and slip the sleeve over the bucket to capture the smoke. Wet the canvas sleeve before putting over the bucket. Add coals from a nearby fire if needed. Try to maintain a smudgy, smoldering fire without flame so that little heat and lots of smoke is produced. It takes some work to regulate the coals so that there is no flame and lots of smoke being produced.

Smoke the hide until it is light brown or until the desired color is obtained. When the inside is smoked, turn the "bag" inside out to smoke the other side of the skin. With heavy smoke the skin should be sufficiently smoked in about 30 minutes to an hour for each side. But the time can vary widely depending on how hot the coals

133

are, the type of punk being used, the wind and other factors. Stay with a hide that is being smoked. Feel the skin periodically to make certain that it is not too hot. If the smoldering coals were to flare up into flame, it could easily burn and ruin the skin.

If a flare up does occur, quickly pull the sleeve off the bucket and pull the hide away from the heat. Settle the flame down to coals before continuing to smoke the hide. Keep a bucket of water handy to sprinkle a little on the flame if needed to cool it down. When smoking hides, keep in mind it is better to over smoke than to under smoke a hide. Smoke the first side until it is bleeding through then turn the skin to smoke the other side.

Smoking Variatons

Normally skins are smoked as described above, but there are a number of other techniques. Some of the methods described below have worked better than others. A person should experiment with different smoking methods to find a method they like best.

A variation of the above method that works good is to use charcoal briquettes in the bucket. Light the charcoal ahead of time and allow it to get burning good before beginning smoking. Add punky wood and put the canvas sleeve over the bucket to capture the smoke as described above.

Another similar method is to cut a hole in the bottom of a bucket and rivet a section of stove pipe into the hole (See *Figure 141*). Charcoal briquettes are lighted as above, or use coals from a fire, and put into a fire pan. When ready, punk is added to the coals in the fire pan and the bucket with the stove pipe is inverted over the coals. The canvas skirt is then put over the stove pipe to capture the smoke. This same method can also be used by placing the coals

on the ground or in a hole in the ground instead of in the fire pan.

A more "high tech" method has, for the author, less than acceptable results; others, however, have had good luck with it. To begin, mount an old propane burner under a small sheep herder style wood stove. Punk is then placed inside the stove, the propane burner lit and the canvas sleeve put over the stack to capture the smoke. This method didn't seem to put out enough smoke and going back to using charcoal briquettes or coals from a fire, as described above, worked better.

Another method is for smoking several skins at a time and is done by placing them inside a small tipi made from willows and covered with some old canvas. Build a fire outside of the tipi and then place hot coals and punk inside the tipi to produce smoke. Additional hot coals and punk may be added as needed to keep the smoke coming. The tipi is closed up except for a small air hole at the bottom and a small opening at the top to help produce a draft. The author has tried this method a couple of times and it took fifteen to twenty hours to produce even a light tan. Other methods work better and faster.

Color and Aroma from Smoke

Many people ask what material to smoke in order to get a certain color and/or aroma. The best answer is to experiment with what is available and find something that produces an acceptable color and aroma. There are several variables to deal with when smoking hides which make it difficult to determine the color the hide will be or even to get the same color twice. The material used, the temperature of the smoke, smoking time, the weather and other factors affect the final color and aroma of the skin; it is a good idea to experiment for different effects.

After experimenting with several different materials for smoking, the author discovered a few

Material used to smoke hides	Color, odor and other information
Quaking aspen punk	Rich yellowish brown, pleasant aroma
Lodge pole pine punk	Bright orange-brown to a rich dark brown. Pleasant aroma. Punk seemed to burn easy and rapidly produced the color.
Douglas Fir punk	Tan to brown color, slow producing the color. Pleasant aroma
Redwood sawdust	Yellow-brown color, very pleasant aroma. Sawdust is slow burning, try redwood chips or bark
Sagebrush - dry wood	Gray to black color, difficult to use since it bursts into flame so easily
Sagebrush foliage	Brown with hint of green or sometimes rich orange brown. Good aroma
Russian olive bark	Rich dark brown, colors rapidly, unpleasant aroma
Willow tree punk	Hot fire gave a dark tan. Cool fire gave a light gray color that took a long time to produce. Aroma OK
Rabbit brush foliage & blossoms	Produced a nice gold color, but fire was difficult to control since it kept bursting into flame, very pungent unpleasant odor.
Elm wood chips	Rich gold brown, pleasant aroma

Table 1

that he would use again and some that he would definitely not use again. Some of the materials are summarized in *Table One* with notes on the results.

After a person finds a suitable smoking material he should try to standardize his smoking methods in an effort to try to get repeatable and uniform results.

WET-SCRAPE BRAIN TANNING

As mentioned above, wet-scrape brain tanning is the process of scraping the hair and grain layer from the hide while the skin is wet. After the hide is fleshed it is usually allowed to soak in water or water and ashes until the hair begins to slip. The hide is then put on a beam and the hair and grain layer is scraped from the hide with a fleshing tool.

Wet-scrape versus dry-scrape: Some contemporary brain tanners prefer the wet-scrape method over dry-scrape, but there are also those who prefer the dry-scrape method. Since both

methods are authentic, a person should learn both, experiment and then decide which method they like best. Each has different advantages and disadvantages for certain applications.

For instance, when wet-scraping, the hide must be scraped within a reasonable amount of time or it will begin to deteriorate. This can be a problem if a person has a busy schedule and is not able to spend enough time to complete the job at one setting. In this case dry-scraping can be advantageous since dried hides can be stored for extended periods and worked on at short intervals as desired until completed. Many part time back-yard tanners would benefit from this advantage.

Large heavy hides that might take considerable work and time to scrape may be best dry-scraped. Small thin skins such as antelope and small deer are sometimes difficult to dry-scrape without tearing them and would benefit from being wet-scraped.

The texture of wet-scraped skins is a little smoother then the texture of dry-scraped skins and if a person has a preference for one or the other then that method should be used.

Dry weather and dry climates are suitable for both wet and dry-scraping but moist weather and climates may be more suitable for wet-scraping hides.

Wet-Scrape Brain Tanning

The first step in wet-scrape brain tanning is to flesh the skin. Do this as described above for dry-scrape brain tanning. Then while the hide is still damp put it in one of the alkali solutions as described below to help loosen the hair and expand the grain layer in preparation for its removal from the skin by wet-scraping. Old tanning books call this next step "liming". If it is not practical to use an alkali solution as below, one can get away with just soaking the skin in water for a few days to loosen the hair and grain layer, however the alkali solution is much more effective.

1. Soak the skins in a solution of ashes and water. Soaking hides in ashes and water was a common Native method to loosen the hair on a hide. To prepare a solution of ashes and water one should try to get just the white ashes from a hardwood fire. If bits of charcoal are included in the solution it most likely will discolor the hides. This has happen to the author and it probably happened many times to the prehistoric Native brain tanner. To avoid the discoloring by charcoal, filter the water and ashes through a course cloth such as burlap.

There is no set amount of ashes to add to water to make a solution because different woods, when burned, have different amounts of lye in their ashes. Many references do not indicate how to determine concentration but simply imply that ashes were put into the solution. A. B. Farnham, in his book, says that the lye should be strong enough to float an egg. Start by stirring ashes into a few gallons of water in a bucket or barrel, let it stand for several hours, filter as above and do the egg test. If the egg fails to float add more ashes. Simple but effective.

When the proper concentration of lye is made add the hide to the clear solution.

2. Soak the skins in lime. Soaking hides in a lime solution is a long established commercial process. Old home chemical and vegetable tanning methods usually call for a lime soak. Use hydrated lime not burnt or caustic lime. The old tanning formulas suggest about eight pounds of hydrated lime per barrel of water (40-50 gallons). One can cut it down proportionately to make a smaller batch. Place hides in the solution and stir several times a day. Deerskins can be left in the lime solution for several days without damage.

3. Soak the skins in washing soda. The use of washing soda (sodium carbonate) in tanning is mentioned briefly in the literature and has been practiced by a few of the author's associates with good results. (See the Ivory Soap® Buckskin section for the amounts to use.) One advantage of using washing soda is that it markedly expands the grain layer making it easier to see and scrape off. Another advantage is that it is not as caustic as commercial lye or lime and would be safe for children to handle.

In each of the above solutions, stir the hides a

few times a day. Check them periodically and when the hair pulls out easily the hide can be removed from the solution.

After the hide has been soaked in one of the above alkali solutions, it is ready to be wet-scraped. To wet-scrape the hair and grain layer from the hide place it over the beam as described in the fleshing step. Lean the body against the hide to hold it, or straddle the beam if it is leaned up to a shed as described. When scraping with the beam against a shed or tree, flop part of the hide behind the beam at the top to secure it while scraping. Begin pushing or pulling the fleshing tool into the skin until it seems to cut into the first layer of skin. The working edge of the tool needs to be dulled, not knife sharp. As the blade is pulled or pushed into the skin it will cut through the grain layer and seem to ride over the skin at a specific layer, pushing the hair and grain layer in front of it. The layer that is being pushed off will be swollen and appear as though too much is being taken off. However, it is difficult to get too thick of a layer since the scraper blade seems to naturally glide along the surface of the lower dermis without cutting into it. Continue scraping the skin carefully, sometimes going back over areas if needed, until the entire grain layer is removed. If the blade is too sharp it could easily cut holes through the skin. If the hair is tight and the skin does not seem to be separating then it may need to be soaked in the alkali solution or water longer. The wet-scrape process takes some practice and experience to master but produces some very nice looking hides when finished.

To remove the alkali from the skin wash it well with water and place it in a barrel of water to soak. Let it soak for about six hours changing the water several times during the soak. Next place the hide into a barrel with about 25 gallons of water to which 1 quart of vinegar has been added to neutralize the remaining alkali. Leave the hide in the vinegar solution overnight or up to 24 hours then rinse thoroughly.

The alkali could also be removed by securing the hide in a stream of water and allowing water to run across it overnight. Or, put it in a barrel of water with a slow stream of water running into it overnight.

After rinsing the vinegar from the skin proceed to the Braining the Skin step and follow the remaining steps in brain tanning.

Making "Buckskin" from Sheep Skin

Sheep skins are usually tanned with the wool on, but they can also be successfully wet-scraped and made into buckskin. During a sheep hide tanning class at a Rabbitstick Rendezvous some of the skins had sat too long and were beginning to lose their wool. So, as an experiment, a student and the author decided to try wet-scraping them. We soaked them in the river and then began to wet-scrape the wool and grain layer from them. The wet-scrape process seemed to be no more difficult than wet-scraping deerskins (these were shorn skins), but since sheep skins are not as tough as deerskins we had to exercise more caution to not tear or cut them. The skins were then brain tanned and smoked; they turned out similar to buckskin. Making "buckskin" from sheepskin might be a way to use skins from which the wool is slipping and may also be a way to obtain inferior buckskin when deerskin is not available. This process deserves more experimentation.

COLORING AND DYEING HIDES

When skin clothing is worn on a daily basis and frequently washed the smoked color will rapidly fade. After a short time it can be almost white. Some people dye their hides after smoking to get a longer lasting color. Alder bark, fir bark, black walnut hulls and other things can be used to dye hides. (See Wearing Buckskins 365 Days a Year section).

The author has experimented primarily with black walnut hulls. Make a black walnut dye solution by crushing the dry hulls into small pieces and either boiling, or just soaking, them in hot water. After the solution cools, a hide can be placed in it either before it is brained or after it is tanned and smoked. Hulls can also be crushed and added to the brain solution so that color is added as the hide is brained. The author prefers to dye the skin in walnut husks after it is tanned and smoked. In that way, it is easier to determine how well the skin is smoked before it is dyed.

Some experimentation is needed to determine how strong to make the solution and how long to soak the hides to achieve the desired color. They may be soaked from just a few hours to a day or two. The color will vary from just a hint of tan to a rich dark brown. The color will also vary depending on the color and intensity of the smoke color. The smoke color can add some interesting variations to the brown color from the walnut husks. After soaking the hides, take them out and check the color. If needed, put them back into the solution to soak longer.

After the desired color is obtained, remove the hides from the solution, rinse well, (a thorough rinsing is required or the hides may drip brown water next time they are washed or get wet), gently squeeze out excess moisture and allow them to dry. As the hides dry, any stiff spots can be worked and softened. The thorough rinsing will lighten the final color a little.

DEERSKIN STRUCTURE AND MAKEUP

In order to better understand the nature of deerskin and to answer a few questions about its structure and how it relates to the tanning process and the quality of the finished buckskin, it is necessary to do a study of deerskin makeup.

Specimens were taken from the hide of a freshly skinned deer and from the same hide and others in different stages of tanning. Some specimens were made into slides, using standard histology techniques, for microscopic study (microscope of 50-100 power). Others were prepared for gross study (studied with the naked eye and with a microscope of 10-30 power).

Deerskin is composed of three basic layers. The outer is known as the epidermis, the next inner layer is the dermis and the third layer under the other two is the hypodermis. The hypodermis is basically fat and connective tissue and is removed during the fleshing step of the tanning process and will not be discussed further. The following text along with the accompanying photographs and drawings will illustrate the basic structure of deerskin dermis and epidermis.

Epidermis

The outer layer of skin, the epidermis, is a microscopically thin layer only a few cells thick. As can be seen in the photomicrograph the nuclei are clearly visible in the cells. This layer consists of millions of individual living epithelial cells. The hair extends about half way into the

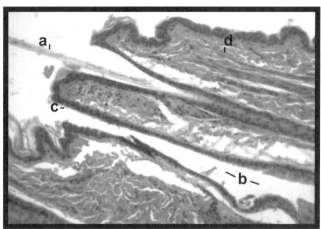

Figure 142. Cross section of deerskin. This piece was cut from a hide that had been soaked for a day or two. It is from about the center of the back. Note that the hairs extend out from about the center of the hides thickness. There is a small amount of fat or membrane visible on the flesh side of the piece of hide. The grain layer extends from the bottom of the roots to the surface.

Figure 143. Photomicrograph of a cross section of deerskin epidermis. This skin specimen was taken from a freshly killed and skinned deer. This photograph shows only a portion of the hair follicles, and not the entire thickness of the skin. (See the drawing at the end of this section for a cross section of the entire thickness of the skin.) The hair in the upper portion of the photo (a) is a fine woolly hair, not the large hairs. The open space through the center of the photo (b) is a hair follicle, or the space where a standard sized hair grows from. The thin dark layer of cells (c) lining the hair follicles is the epidermis. Note how it is not only on the outer portion of the skin but also lines the inside of the hair follicles. The lighter colored tissue (d) is the dermis. Photo by Jane Bennett-Munro M.D.

skins thickness and is an appendage of the epidermis. Since the epidermis lines each hair follicle to the root, the layer is very convoluted. New epidermal cells are generated from the lower surface of the layer. Older cells on the surface eventually die and form a thin keratin layer on the surface of the skin.

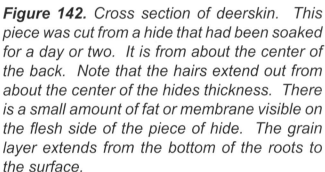

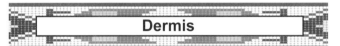

Dermis

The bulk of the first two layers of skin is dermis which lies just beneath the epidermal layer. The dermal layer consists mostly of protein (collagen) fibers tightly interwoven with each other. It also contains blood vessels, nerve endings, sebaceous glands, smooth muscle, fiberblasts and other components.

Throughout most of the hide the hair extends out from about the center of the hide dividing the dermal layer into two distinct layers: (a) The layer of dermis that surrounds the hair follicles and (b) the layer of dermis that lies below the hair follicles. These two layers are about the

same thickness except that in the thinner parts of the hide (flanks, belly, legs and rump) the dermis lying below the hair follicles is sometimes considerably thinner. The thickness of the dermis around the hair follicles seems to be fairly uniform throughout the hide.

In tanning, the dermis surrounding the hair follicles is usually distinguished from the rest of the dermis by being called the "grain layer." The difference in behavior of these two layers, during skin processing and tanning, warrants this somewhat artificial distinction. These two layers will be discussed and described separately.

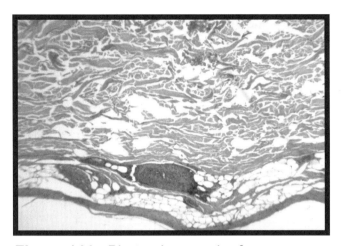

Figure 144. Photomicrograph of a cross section of deerskin lower dermis. This skin specimen was taken from a freshly killed and skinned deer. This photograph shows the dermis that lies below the hair follicles. The specimen is cut very thin so the long fibrous nature of the dermis is not clearly visible. The globular material at the bottom of the picture is adipose or fat tissue (hypodermis). Below that is muscle or membrane tissue. Photo by Jane Bennett-Munro, MD.

Grain Layer of the Dermis

Grain is technically not a part of the skin but it is the quality or texture of the outer surface of the skin when tanned. When the hair is removed from a hide, the arrangement of the hair follicles gives the hide a certain characteristic surface pattern and texture. This pattern and texture is called the grain. Different animal species have their own distinguishing patterns giving each kind of hide its aesthetic qualities. Since it is the hair follicles and their arrangement that produces the grain patterns, the dermis that surrounds the hair follicles is called the grain layer. (Note: The epidermis is also a part of the grain layer).

The most obvious structure in the grain layer is the hair follicles and roots. These take up most of the room in the grain layer, in fact the thickness of dermis between many hair roots is less than the thickness of the hairs. The hairs protrude out so thickly that they seem to almost all touch each other. When the hairs are pulled or lightly scraped from a soaked hide, the grain layer collapses (because of the loss of hair root volume) taking up less than half of the thickness of the hide. If the hide is allowed to dry with only minimal working (rawhide) the grain layer will dry into a thin but very tough layer.

The bulk of the dermis in the grain layer is composed of collagen fibers. Also included in with the fibers are oil producing sebaceous glands, blood vessels, nerve endings, erectile muscle which causes the hairs to stand on end, fiberblasts or cells that produce collagen fibers and other structures. At the juncture of the dermis with the epidermis there are small undulations known as papillae. This region of the grain layer is known as the papillary dermis, the rest of the dermis is termed reticular dermis.

The collagen fibers in the grain layer appear to be finer and more tightly woven than the fibers of the lower dermis, and appear to be woven the tightest at the top of the dermis, producing the smooth surface on grain leather. The collagen fibers also seem to align somewhat vertically and circularly around the hair follicles.

Lower Dermis

The dermal layer that lies below the hair follicles is also composed mostly of a network of collagen fibers. These fibers are made up of bundles of smaller fibers producing a fiber that is coarser than the fibers in the grain layer. These fibers are hopelessly entangled and tightly matted together. They run in all directions from each other but are organized basically horizontally with the hide. The collagen in the lower dermis merges into the collagen in the grain layer with no distinct point of juncture. The main distinguishing difference between the two layers is that the bottom of the hair follicles defines the bottom of the grain layer and the

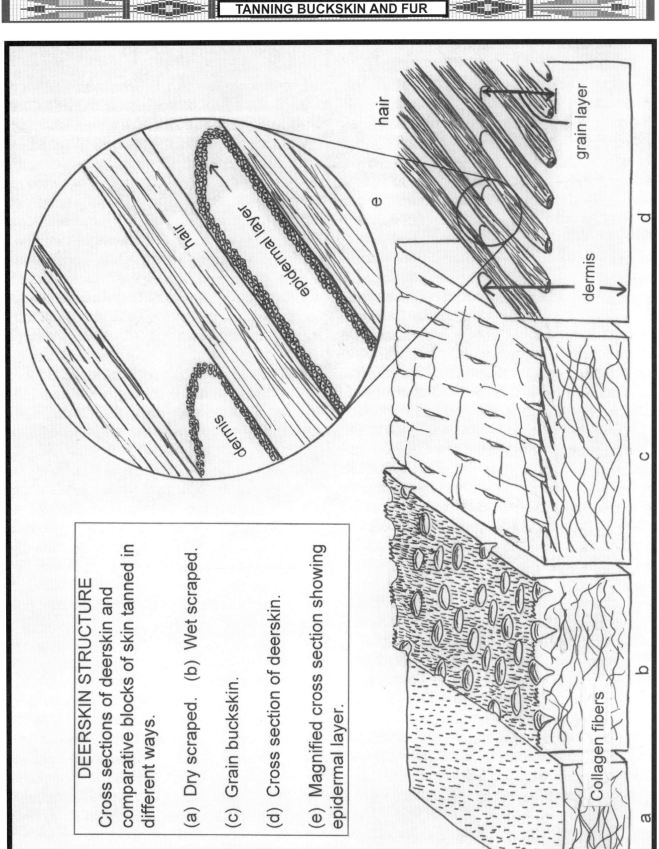

DEERSKIN STRUCTURE
Cross sections of deerskin and comparative blocks of skin tanned in different ways.

(a) Dry scraped. (b) Wet scraped.

(c) Grain buckskin.

(d) Cross section of deerskin.

(e) Magnified cross section showing epidermal layer.

Figure 145

top of the lower dermal layer.

Figure 145 illustrates deer skin structure - simplified for clarity. (a) Dry-scraped brain tanned. The grain layer of collagen has been completely removed from below the roots and the surface texture is uniform. (b) Wet-scraped brain tanned. The grain layer separates through the bulbs of the hair follicle leaving a small portion of the grain layer on the finished hide. Bases of the hair follicle (holes) are sometimes visible. (c) Grain buckskin. Skin tanned with the collapsed grain layer attached. The surface of the grain layer is smooth but forms a crinkled pattern. Flattened hair follicles are sometimes visible. (d) Cross section of deer skin, hairs originate from about half way into the skin. (e) Magnified cross section, showing thin epidermal layer lining the hair follicles and covering the outer layer of the dermis.

The difference between the wet-scraped surface texture and dry-scraped surface texture results from the different ways the grain layer is removed from the hide. A third texture results when the hide is tanned without removing the grain layer.

The usual goal in dry-scraping is to remove all the hair and surrounding tissue to the roots of the hair. As seen in the illustrations of the deerskin cross sections this would entail scraping away most if not all of the dermis surrounding the hair follicles or grain layer. This leaves just the lower dermis to be tanned. The hair side surface of a dry-scraped and brain-tanned hide appears much like a carpet with an even pile. This uniform texture is formed by the collagen fibers being cut with a sharp tool and standing up from the surface.

A different and more complicated set of circumstances is involved in the wet-scrape process that produces the distinctive surface characteristics (smoother than dry-scrape) of the wet-scraped hide.

When wet-scraping a properly soaked hide, one can feel a definite level at which the blade of the scraper comes to while scraping off the outer tissues of the skin. It feels and looks as though one layer is being peeled from another at a specific junction but this is not the case. Wet-scraping takes only part of the grain layer leaving the lower dermis with a portion of the grain layer still attached. The dermis surrounding the hair follicles has a very tough tightly matted surface. The remainder of the collagen fibers that surround the hair follicles are possibly aligned more vertically and are not as tightly matted around the hair follicles. They gradually merge into the coarser, more tightly entangled and more horizontally aligned fibers of the lower dermal layer.

When the blade of the wet-scrape tool is scraped against the hide it cuts through the grain layer and begins to ride on the surface of the more horizontally matted lower dermis. As the tool is pushed along it appears that it separates the grain layer by pulling it apart and separating the fibers through the bulbs of the hair follicles where the dermis seems to be the thinnest and weakest. This leaves a small amount of the grain layer attached to the lower dermis. In addition, aside from the chemical action on the hide, alkali solutions swell or expand the grain layer making it more visible and easier to scrape away from the remaining dermis.

Under gross microscopic examination of the surface of a wet-scraped brain-tanned hide, it can be seen that the deeper dermis is more matted down and does not seem to be raised up or trimmed off as much as in the dry-scraped hide. The fibers that are protruding from the surface seem to be mostly the finer collagen fibers that separated from around the hair follicles in the grain layer. They are raised up sometimes in somewhat of a circular pattern indicating the structure of the hair follicles. In wet-scraped antelope and domestic sheep hides, the circular patterns are more pronounced, indicating dermis that had surrounded the hair follicles. Remnants of hair root holes are also sometimes visible in the surface of wet-scraped brain tanned deer hides, indicating that the separation of the two layers is somewhere above the bottom of the hair roots. Some of the finer grain layer collagen fibers are matted down forming a tighter surface texture to the hide than the dry-scraped hide surface. This would explain the smoother look of the wet-scraped hides. It may also have something to do with the brain penetration being more difficult in wet-scraped hides.

Traditionally it has been contended that the outer layers of the hide (epidermis and grain layer) must be removed before authentic buckskin can be made. It has usually been said that the skin is very difficult to break and cannot be made soft if these layers are left on. But if properly brain-tanned and broken, the skin can be successfully tanned with the grain layer attached and be made very soft. This has been demonstrated by some who are experimenting with the process (see Brain Tanning with the Grain Layer Attached below). The surface texture of the skin resembles commercially tanned leather. It has a smooth, not suede, surface and a definite texture or pattern.

The difficulty in tanning the skin with the grain on lies in the different stretch ability of the two layers of the skin. The lower dermis is more elastic than the dermis surrounding the hair follicles. When the grain layer is left in place the hide does not stretch as easily making breaking more difficult. If the hide is not thoroughly and completely broken the grain will be thick and will dry stiff. Microscopic examination of cross sections of hides improperly broken this way show that this stiff layer is composed of the collapsed dried epidermis and grain layer. Flattened sebaceous glands and hair follicles are sometimes clearly visible in this layer. If a hide with the grain on is tanned and thoroughly worked it can be made soft. Examination of these hides show that the top grain or slick layer is thin and soft. Gross microscopic examination shows that most of the grain layer collagen fibers have been properly separated and fluffed up making the hide soft. Only the very surface tissues and fibers are not completely separated leaving the smooth grain surface.

Microscopic studies, done by the author, have indicated that hides tanned with the "grain layer" attached sometimes still retain epidermal tissue. Cross sections of hides soaked in lime for over four days and soft wet-scraped to remove only the hair clearly showed epidermal tissue still attached to the dermis of the skin. After breaking and softening by mainly stretching, the skin cross sections again showed attached epidermal tissues.

BRAIN TANNING WITH THE GRAIN LAYER ATTACHED

Normally, to properly tan buckskin the grain layer must be removed, but at a Rabbitstick Rendezvous the author saw several skins with the grain layer left on that were successfully tanned by a young woman named Lynx. The skins were soft and the attached grain layer formed an attractive crinkle pattern on the skin.

When asked about it, she said she soaked the skins in water and wood ash and then removed the hair by lightly scraping and plucking, leaving the outer or grain layer in place. She then brained the skins as usual and laced them into a frame. She softened them by extensive pushing of the skins with her hands, from the hair side, and scraping and working them thoroughly from the flesh side with tools such as a wooden breaking stick and a slate ulu.

She worked and pushed the skins until they

were completely dry and soft. The skins were then smoked as usual and a mixture of pitch, beeswax and neatsfoot oil was rubbed onto the hair side to help the skin shed water. She had made a nice backpack from some of the skins which she said protected her gear from getting wet in a storm.

Brain tanning with the grain layer left on the skin would be worthy of further experimentation.

Finished skins have a different texture than either wet-scraped or dry-scraped brain tanned skins, which not only provides variety but may be superior for some applications as mentioned above.

Some skins tanned by Charles Robbins in his soap tanning experiments had the epidermis and grain layer attached. See the Ivory® Soap Buckskin section.

FURS SKIN TANNING

The American Indians left the hair on some of their skins when they were tanned. This provided them with blankets, robes and material for clothing. Buffalo, deer, elk and many fur animals were tanned this way.

The steps in brain tanning a skin with fur or hair on are about the same as brain tanning buckskin except that the hair removal steps are not done and the braining, breaking and drying steps are modified to avoid damage to the hair or fur.

1. The first step is to clean and flesh the skin. If the skin is fresh, wash by hand with mild soap and lukewarm water, rinse well and carefully squeeze, but don't wring, to remove excess water. Flesh as described below. If the skin is dry, soak it in water for a few hours or overnight to saturate and relax it. Then wash with soap and water, rinse and proceed to fleshing. A good scrub brush and some mild soap or shampoo may be needed to clean up sheep skins or other skins with thick fur or hair.

Put the skin over a fleshing beam, as described in the buckskin tanning section, hold the skin by leaning the body against it, and with a fleshing tool push the flesh off the hide. Small hides may need to be placed on a flat surface and held with one hand and fleshed with the other using an end fleshing tool (See *Tools for Tan-*

ning section).

For best results with sheep pelts, start with clean, freshly skinned pelts, cool them immediately by spraying them with cold water or allowing them to cool over night in cool weather. Fat on sheep pelts left lying around in the heat of the day will soon begin to rot and will cause the wool to slip. Rapid cooling will prevent this and will also solidify the fat making it easier to scrape from the hide. If desired, trim off the legs, flanks and rough edges.

2. Braining the skin. Mash up a small quantity of animal brains with about half their volume of water to give the mixture a thin, pasty consistency. This mixture is heated to about 100 F. Work the brain mixture into the skin by rubbing with a smooth flat stone. Continue working the mixture until the skin is completely saturated. Fold the skin, flesh sides together, roll it up and store it in a plastic bag at room temperature for about six hours for small skins such as rabbits etc. or overnight for larger animal skins such as coyote, sheep, and others.

Note: Some like to tan deer and elk skins with the hair on by lacing the skin into a frame and rubbing the brains into the flesh side of the hide. It is then broken and dried in the frame also (See below).

144

3. Breaking and drying the skin. Take the skin out of the bag and unroll it with the flesh side up. Scrape off the excess brains and allow the skin to start drying. As it begins to dry, start breaking and softening it. This is done by laying the skin on a soft surface such as a rug, or piece of carpet, and repeatedly scraping the flesh side with a breaking tool.

It works well to scrape the skin by pushing the stick from the center of the skin out to the edge. Or, pull the tool from the center of the skin towards the body. Rotate the skin a little each time and scrape the tool in every direction to completely work the whole skin.

Check the skin periodically as it dries and work it a little each time. When it begins to turn milky white and gets velvety as it is scraped and stretched, it is at the right stage to soften. When the skin reaches this stage, continue scraping and stretching the skin at regular intervals until it is completely dry and velvety soft.

The skin could also be broken by rubbing it over a staking tool in a manner similar to shining shoes (See *Figure 152*). See section *Tools for Tanning* for instructions on how to make breaking or staking tools. Once the skin is dry, brush and fluff the fur and finish by trimming any rough edges. It is now ready to be smoked. If breaking a deer skin or similar size skin with the hair or fur on, it can be laced into a frame, and a

staking pole used to stretch and work the hide until it is dry and soft.

4. Smoking the skin. The skin can be smoked as described in the section on smoking buckskin; the only difference is that just the flesh side needs to be smoked. After smoking, the skin may be carefully washed by hand with mild soap to clean any remaining brain residue from the hair. As it dries gently work the skin and fluff the hair to attain its full softness again.

Brain tanning buffalo hides with the hair on produces authentic robes but involves quite a bit more work than tanning sheep hides or other smaller hides as explained in this section. It is recommended that a person tan several smaller skins and furs to get a good feel for the process before tackling a buffalo hide. The tanning steps described in this section will work for tanning a buffalo, but because of the size of the hides the tanning steps need to be modified to some extent just to be able to accomplish them.

Jim Miller, a friend of the author's from Michigan, is an experienced buffalo hide brain tanner. His buffalo hides are nicely done in the traditional way. In 1997, he published a booklet on brain tanning with a section devoted to brain tanning buffalo robes with the hair on. It is recommended that the reader obtain his booklet for more details on tanning buffalo hides. (see *References* for address.)

TOOLS FOR TANNING

Fleshing Tools

A fleshing beam (and/or dehairing beam) can be made from a 6 inch diameter log about five or six feet long that is smoothed and evenly rounded on one side. It can be mounted on a stand at waist height or it can be leaned up to a shed or tree as shown in *Figure 146*. To use,

the hide is placed over the beam and the body is pushed against the hide to hold it while the flesh or hair is pushed of with a fleshing tool. To use the beam, mounted against a tree or building, just lay the hide over it with part of the hide overlapping between the beam and the tree. Then scrape the flesh from the hide by pulling the fleshing tool down the hide. The hide will need to be adjusted as it is cleaned so that

Figure 146. Two types of beams used for fleshing and dehairing.

the part being fleshed is directly on top of the beam.

Using a waist beam to flesh a hide is illustrated in *Figure 147*.

There are a number of different types of fleshing tools that can be made or purchased. The ones illustrated in *Figure 148* are all home made. The two on the left are for fleshing hides over a beam. The bone ones are similar to the bone scrapers made by early Native Americans and are used when hides are stretched in frames or pegged to the ground.

A tool similar to the bone tools can be made from a sturdy butcher knife. Grind the sharp edge to dull it and grind the point off to square off the end. This end should be slightly rounded and then beveled as shown and small teeth ground into the rounded end. This tool is used

Figure 147.

Figure 148. Fleshing tools.

in a hacking manner to remove flesh from a hide that is stretched out on the ground or in a frame.

The other fleshing tools shown in the picture are made from scrap metal. For a heavy duty scraper get a piece of scrap steel about 18 - 20 inches long by 1 1/2 inches wide and 1/4 inch thick. Grind the center portion (between the handles) to a beveled edge of approximately 45 degrees. This edge should be sharp but slightly dulled so that it won't cut the hide when in use. Leave the opposite edge squared; sometimes the squared edge is used in fleshing and dehairing, also. Cut four pieces of hardwood and drill them, and the tool, and mount the pieces of wood on the ends for handles as shown in the photograph. Scrap buckskin can be wrapped on the ends for handles instead of the wood. This scraping tool is also very good for wet-scraping hair and the grain layer from skin.

Lighter fleshing tools can be made from lighter scrap steel as shown in the photo. These tools are handy for wet-scraping a hide after it has been brained to cleanup bits of flesh, membrane and grain layer that were missed during the first scrapings. These lighter tools do not need the wood handles but it helps to round off the edges or to wrap the ends with buckskin.

A simple tool used to scrape membrane from a hide as it dries can be made from a hacksaw blade; use a fine toothed blade. See *Figure 153* for a photo of the tool. Cut an inch and a half diameter stick about five inches long for a handle. Cut a notch in each end and drill holes into the ends of the handle. Attach one end of the blade with a screw, bend the blade to the other end and attach with another screw. After hides are tanned and broken this tool can be used to remove any remaining membrane by scraping the flesh side of the hide with the saw toothed edge of the saw blade.

Dry Hide Scrapers

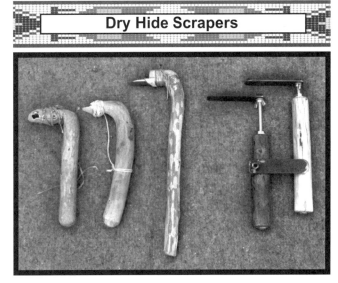

Figure 149. Scrapers for dry scraping the hair from dried hides.

The first two hide scrapers in *Figure 149* have flintknapped stone blades lashed to wooden handles similar to the tools used by the early Native Americans. The handles were often antler or wood. The next scraper has a wood handle similar to the primitive one but has a steel blade. To make this scraper find a stick with a 90 degree bend or a branch that can be cut to 90 degrees. A steel blade can be made from an old file that is about 1 to 1 1/2 inches wide. Break or cut a 4 inch piece from it, round one end and sharpen just the top of the blade and lash it to the handle as shown in *Figure 149*. The last two scrapers shown are made by attaching steel blades to carriage bolts with

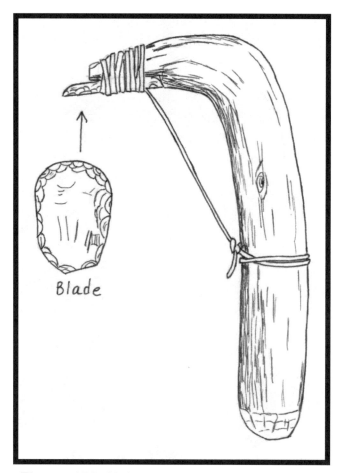

Blade

Figure 150. Hair scraper with a stone blade. Flintknap a stone blade shaped like the one above and lash it with a rawhide or buckskin strip to a handle made from wood or antler as shown.

wooden handles. The front of the blades are ground as previously described. The wing nuts provide for easy removal of the blades for sharpening or for storage safety. See *Figure 151* for details of making the scraping tool.

Shown in *Figure 151* is an extremely sturdy tool. The author has made and sold dozens of these and they stand up to a lot of scraping. The blade is made from hardened steel blanks that may be ordered from a factory that makes blades. Order them 5 1/4 inches long, 1 1/4 inches wide and 1/8 inch thick. The factory pre-drills holes in one end and nuts may be welded to the blade to make attachment to the handle easier. Then grind the blades to shape with an angle grinder.

(As seen in the drawing and photo, round the front of the blade and only grind the top of the blade). After grinding the blades, sharpen them with a whet stone. The handle is made by drilling a hole through a wooden branch of the proper diameter and length and inserting a 3/8, 10 - 12 inch long carriage bolt through it. Tighten down a nut and washer to hold the wood on securely then attach the handle to the blade. The wing nut is then tightened against a lock

Figure 151. Modern dry scraping tool made from steel.

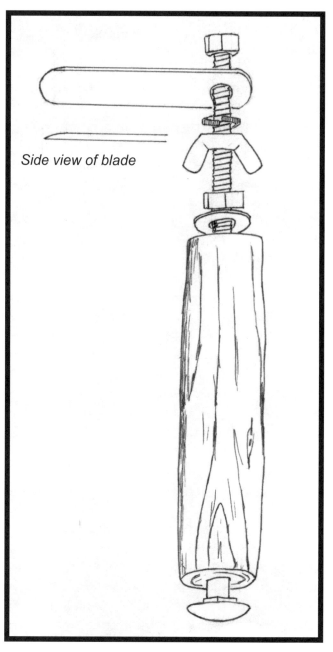

Side view of blade

washer to the blade and it is ready for use.

Staking Tools

Figure 152. *Staking a hide over a disc staking tool.*

A staking tool has an edge over which hides can be stretched as they dry to help break and soften them. A two by four or two by six can be shaped to an edge and mounted on a stand at about waist hieght, or a metal edge can be mounted on the top of the board to break the hide. Another way to make a good staking tool is to weld an old disk onto a stand as in *Figure 152*. For both tools be sure to sand or grind off any sharp edges that would tear the hide or catch a persons hands or fingers as they work on the hide. To use, pull and stretch the hide up and down over the tool in a manner similar to shining shoes with a rag.

Figure 153. *Staking tools.*

A hand staking tool for frame staking can be made from any stick or pole about two inches in diameter and about four feet long. One end is well rounded and the other is beveled to an edge but rounded, so that there are no sharp corners to tear the hide. This tool is used to stretch and break a hide while it is in the frame as described in the Breaking and Drying Skins section. Small hand stakers as shown in *Figure 153* may also be made from sticks for use in softening sheepskins, rabbit skins and other small fur skins.

OTHER TANNING METHODS

Ivory® Soap Buckskin

By experimentation and studying old soap tanning methods Charles Robbins developed this Ivory® Soap tanning method a number of years ago when he was a volunteer leader of a Varsity Boy Scout Unit. He wanted a tanning method that used easily obtainable supplies and that children and young adults could be turned loose with without the concern of their handling hazardous or caustic materials.

The buckskins he produces with this method are velvety soft. His steps are:

FLESHING

Submerge the hide in a container of warm water and allow it to soak overnight.

Remove the hide from the water and hang it over a fleshing beam and let it begin to dry. While the hide is still damp remove all fat, flesh and membrane by scraping (See *Tools for Tanning* section for different types of fleshing tools).

HAIR REMOVAL

For each 3 gallons of warm water used add 1 cup of washing soda (obtainable in the laundry section of grocery stores). Submerge the hide in this solution and keep it in a warm place for a few days. Stir the hide at least twice a day. When the hair can easily be scraped off remove the hide from the solution, place it over a fleshing beam and scrape the hair and grain layer off with the fleshing tools as described above. If there are spots where the hair does not come off easily, return the hide to the solution for another day or two and then scrape again.

TANNING

Dissolve one large, two medium or four small bars of Ivory® soap in a gallon of boiling water. Add two more gallons of water to the soap solution. The solution should be warm but not too hot to the touch. Submerge the hide in this solution. Keep in a warm place and stir at least twice a day. After soaking the hide for about 4 days in warm weather, or 6 days in cool weather,

take it out of the soap solution. Rinse the hide lightly and hang it over something and let it begin to dry.

BREAKING

As the hide dries work it over a staking tool or stretch and pull it around a rope or cable (as previously described in the Braining section) until it is completely dry and soft. Chuck said he has better luck breaking the hides while they first dry rather than drying them and re-wetting and breaking later.

SMOKING

The last step is to smoke the hides. His smoking methods are similar to the previously described Smoking Skins methods in the brain tanning section.

Some notes about soap tanning: The author experimented with the above soap tanning method and offers the following observations:

A. Both the washing soda and Ivory® soap expanded the grain layer making it more visible and easy to wet-scrape off.

B. One advantage of soap tanning over brain tanning is that once the hair is removed the hide smells fresh like the Ivory® soap, through the rest of the process. It does not seem to grow bacteria or develop a bad odor. One concern about brain tanning is that the brain solution is a good growth media for bacteria and there is a small possibility of getting an infection in the hands. This would be less likely using the soap tanning method. The finished hide (before smoking) retains a slight Ivory® soap odor.

C. Since no bad odors develop from soap tanning, flies and hornets are not as attracted to the hides as they are to hides being tanned with brains. This is a slight concern since the author and others have on occasion been stung while brain tanning hides.

D. Tanning with Ivory® soap seems to be no more difficult than traditional brain tanning methods. Soap tanned skins need to be smoked for the same reason that brain tanned skins are smoked. After smoking, the soap tanned skins were indistinguishable from brain tanned skins.

E. Another brand of soap that had about the same main ingredients as Ivory® Soap was tried and the results were similar. The main ingredients in Ivory® soap are vegetable and animal fats along with small amounts of preservatives and fragrance. Other brands of soap that contain mainly fats would probably work, but brands that are formulated from synthetic ingredients or detergents may not work as well. Some experimentation would be necessary to determine if a particular soap worked.

F. Even though soap tanning is not an authentic Native American skill it was practiced earlier in our nations history by industrious woodsmen and home tanners using homemade soap. It is a good alternative to brain tanning if brains are not available or if a person just does not want to use brains.

G. Waste soap tanning solutions are not hazardous and can be disposed of by draining to an individual or city sewage disposal system.

Commercial Tanning Kits

Authentic looking buckskin can be produced using a tanning kit. Flesh and scrape the hair and grain layer from the skin as described earlier or as directed in the kit instructions. Then tan the skin according to the instructions. At the end of the tanning process, break the skin by working it over the rope until it is dry and flannel soft. Smoke the skin as described above to produce the authentic aroma and color.

There are a number of commercial tanning kits available. Some use acids and chromium solutions, while others use oils and creams that are rubbed onto the skin. These work fine if the instructions are followed. But if a person wants a less expensive chemical method, there is a simple old method using sulfuric acid that also does a nice job. The following is only one of several acid tanning formulas.

Acid Tan Method

This tanning method works well on skins tanned with either the hair or fur on or off. When tanning with the hair on, the acid sets the hair or fur and keeps it from slipping. When tanning hides with the hair or fur attached, flesh as described above, skip soaking in the alkali solution and go to step Number Two below. If the hair is to be removed follow all steps below.

1. Soak the skin in one of the alkali solutions according to the instructions in the Braining section of this book. Then remove the hair and the grain layer as described in that section.

2. Battery acid (sulfuric acid) can be obtained from farm supply or automotive batteries stores. Do not use acid from old batteries since it may contain lead and the acid concentration will be unknown.

Mix a tanning solution as follows:
        1 gallon of water
        4 ounces battery acid
        1 pound salt (rock salt or water softener
            salt)

Mix the water and salt then slowly pour the acid into solution while stirring.

Soak the fleshed and cleaned hide in the solution for 3-10 (sometimes as many as 14) days depending on the size of the hide. Agitate for five minutes twice daily. Small thin hides will tan in less time than large thick ones.

3. After tanning is complete remove the skin and thoroughly rinse it in cool running water. Add a few tablespoons of baking soda to 5-10 gallons of water, plunge the skin in this solution for a few minutes to help neutralize the remaining acid. Then again thoroughly rinse in running water with agitation.

4. The skin can now be allowed to start drying. As the skin begins to dry lightly rub in neatsfoot oil or tanning oil and work the skin by stretching until it is completely dry and soft. The skin should be broken using the same methods as described for brain tanning hides with either the hair on or off.

Using a small breaking stick, lay the skin out on a flat soft surface and rub with the stick to stretch and soften, or the skin may also be broken over a staking tool. (See *Tool for Tanning* section for description of tools)

ABOUT THE AUTHOR

Evard H. Gibby grew up on a farm near Burley, Idaho where he gained a love for the outdoors. In the late 1960's he began experimenting with hide tanning using a kit purchased from a mail order house. About the same time as a student at Brigham Young University he obtained a copy of Larry Dean Olsen's book "Outdoor Survival Skills" and began learning primitive and survival skills. During that summer his two younger brothers and a neighbor boy were willing students and he took these three boys hiking and camping in the nearby Idaho hills to work on primitive and survival skills.

Evard enjoys camping with his family, nature study, primitive skills and photography. Evard graduated from Brigham Young University, Provo, Utah in 1972. He has worked as an Environmental Health Specialist for the Public Health Department in Twin Falls, Idaho since 1979.

Evard has been involved with a unique Specialty Explorer Post of the Boy Scouts of America which specializes in teaching the youth post members, skills practiced by the native peoples of America.

He has also taught primitive skills through the Continuing Education Department of a local college and at various Rendezvous including the annual Rabbit Stick Rendezvous in Rexburg, Idaho.

Evard and his wife Paula live in Kimberly Idaho and have five sons and one daughter. He is the author of two other books: *How to Tan Skins The Indian Way* and *How to Make Primitive Pottery* also available from Eagle's View Publishing.

THIS BOOK

EVARD H. GIBBY

The process by which this book was written
took a lot of time.
I've had to read and write and read and write
and alter every line.

Thoughts have come into my mind;
I've put them to the pen,
I've thought about them all the time
and changed them now and then.

Each thought and phrase was difficult
to put in final form,
and information sometimes came
in a mighty storm.

I've put it down as fast as I can
I've wonder'd if it's right,

because it seems this happens
only in the dark of night.

And as I've worked and toiled,
a little every day,
the book began to take it's shape
my labors finally pay.

But if I'd known just what a chore
it was to write this book,
I think I would have balked a little
and took a second look.

But now it's done and on the page,
I hope it's halfway good
and if you've read this mighty mess,
I hope you've understood.

INDEX

REFERENCES

Academic American Encyclopedia Vol. 12, Grolier Incorporated, Danbury, CT. 1989

Almy, Marion M. and George M. Luer. *Guide to the Prehistory of Historic Spanish Point in Southwest Florida*, Historic Spanish Point, 500 North Tamiami Trail, Osprey, FL 34229. 1993

Baldwin, Gordon C. *The Ancient Ones, Basket Makers and Cliff Dwellers of the Southwest*, W.W. Norton Company Inc., New York, NY. 1963

Bauer, Helen. *California Indian Days*, Doubleday and Company Inc., Garden City, NY. 1963

Belitz, Larry. *Step by Step Brain Tanning the Sioux Way*, HCR 52 Box 176, Hot Springs, SD 57747. 1973

Broder, Patric Janis. *Shadows on Glass, The Indian Works of Ben Wittick*, Roman and Littlefield Publishers Inc., 8705 Bollman Place, Savage, Maryland 20763. 1990

Byers, D. Stanley. *Chopped Finger or Cut Throat: Styles, Construction, and Identification of Nineteenth Century Plains Indian Clothing*, A Masters Thesis Submitted To The Graduate Faculty, Central State University, Edmond, Oklahoma. 1990

Capps, Benjaman. *The Old West - the Indians*, Time Life Books, New York. 1973

Catlin, George. *Letters and Notes on the Manners and Customs of the North American Indians, Vol I and II,* originally published 1841, Ross and Haines Inc., Minneapolis. 1965

Catlin, George. *Letters and Notes on the North American Indians,* Edited and with an Introduction by Michael M. Mooney, Clarkston N. Potter Inc., Publisher, New York. 1975

Columbus, Christopher. *The Log of Christopher Columbus*, Translated by Robert H. Fuson, International Marine Publishing Company, Camden, Maine. 1492 (Translated 1987)

Conn, Richard. *Native American Art in the Denver Art Museum*, The Denver Art Museum, University of Washington Press, Seattle and London. 1979

Curtis, Edward S. *Portraits from North American Indian Life*, Outerbridge and Lazard Inc., Promontory Press, New York, NY. 1972

D'Azevedo, Warren L., Volume Editor. *Handbook of North American Indians Volume 11,* The Great Basin, Smithsonian Institution, Washington. 1986

Davis, Christopher. *North American Indian*, Hamlyn Publishing Group Limited, London and New York. 1970

Drucker, Philip. *Indians of the Northwest Coast,* The American Museum of Natural History, The Natural History Press, Garden, NY. 1963

Dumas, David. *Handbook of North American Indians Volume 5,* Smithsonian Institution, U.S., Government Printing Office, Washington, DC 20402. 1984

Eagle's View Patterns, 6756 North Fork Road, Liberty, Utah 84310.

Edholm, Steven and Tamara Wilder. *Wet-Scrape Braintanned Buckskin: A Practical Guide To Home Tanning And Use*, Paleotechnics, Boonville, California. 1997

Erdoes, Richard. *Native Americans - The Pueblos,* Sterling Publishing Co. Inc., New York. 1983

Ewers, John. *Blackfoot Crafts*, Department of The Interior, United States Indian Service, Haskel Institute. 1945

Ewers, John C. *The Blackfoot Raiders of the Northern Plains*, University of Oklahoma Press. 1958

Farnham, Albert B. *Home Tanning and Leather Making Guide*, A. R. Harding, Columbus, Ohio.

Fecteau, Susan. *Primitive Indian Dresses*, Frontier Printing Inc., Cheyenne, Wyoming 82001. 1979

Fleming, Paula and Judith Luskey. *The North American Indians in Early Photographs*, Harper and Row Publishers, New York. 1986

Funaro, Diana. *The Yestermorrow Cloths Book*, Chilton Book Company, Radnor, PA. 1976

Fuson, Robert H. *The Log of Christopher Columbus*, International Marine Publishing Company, Camden, Maine. 1987

Gibby, Evard H. *How to Tan Skins The Indian Way*, Eagles View Publishing Company, A WestWind, Inc. Company, 6756 North Fork Road, Liberty, Utah. 1991

Gidley, Mick. *The Vanishing Race, Selections from Edwards Curtis - The North American Indians*, Toplinger Publishing Co. Inc., New York, NY. 1977

Gridley, Marion E. *American Indian Tribes*, Dodd, Mead and Company, New York. 1974

Hail, Barbara A. *Hau, Kola! Plains Indian Collection*, Heffenreffer Museum Of Anthropology, Brown University, Bristol, RI. 1980

Haire, Francis H. *The American Costume Book*, A. S. Barns and Company. 1937

Hamre, Ida and Hanne Meedom. *The Structure and Development of Cloths from Other Cultures*, Adam and Charles Black, London. 1980

Hartman, Sheryl. *Indian Clothing of the Great Lakes: 1740-1840*, Eagles View Publishing Company, A WestWind, Inc. Company, 6756 North Fork Road, Liberty, Utah. 1988

Hassrick, Royal B. *The Sioux,* The University of Oklahoma Press, Publishing Division of the University. 1964

Heizer, Robert F., Volume Editor. *Handbook of North American Indians Volume 8*. Smithsonian Institution, U.S. Government Printing Office, Washington, DC 20402. 1978

Helm, June, Volume Editor. *Handbook of North American Indians Volume 6*, Smithsonian Institution, U.S. Government Printing Office, Washington, DC 20402. 1981

Hoebel, E. Adamson. *The Cheyenne's - The Indians of the Great Plains*, Holt Rineholt and Winston, New York, Chicago, San Francisco. 1960

Hoshaw, Robert W. *Spanish Moss*, The World Book Encyclopedia, World Book Inc., Chicago. 1983

Hungry Wolf, Adolf and Beverly Blackfoot. *Craftworkers Book,* Good Medicine Books Skookumchuck, BC, Canada. 1977

Hungry Wolf, Adolf. *Traditional Dress, Knowledge and Methods of the Old-Time Clothings*, Book Publishing Company, Summertown, TN, USA, Good Medicine Books, Skookumchuck, BC, Canada. 1990

Hunter, John D. *Manners and Customs Of the Indian Tribes*, Ross and Haines Inc., Minneapolis, Minnesota. 1957

James, George Wharton. *Indian Blankets and Their Makers*, Tudar Publishing Co., New York 1937. Copyright 1914 By Edith Farnsworth Van Rees Press, New York.

Janetski, Joel C. *Indians of Yellowstone Park*, Bonnevile Books, University of Utah Press, Salt Lake City, UT. 1987

Knoph, Alford A. and Josephy, Alvin M. *The Indian Heritage of America*, New York. 1968

Koch, Ronald P. *Dress Clothing of The Plains Indians*, Normon, University of Oklahoma Press. 1977

La Farge, Oliver. *Pictorial History of the American Indian*, Crown Publishers Inc., New York, New York. 1956

Lowie, Robert H. *The Crow Indian*, Holt, Rinehart and Winston, New York. 1935 and 1956

Lowie, Robert H. *Indians of the Plains*, American Museum of Natural History, University of Nebraska Press. 1954

Mails, Thomas E. *The Mystic Warriors of the Plains*, Double Day and Company Inc., Garden City, New York. 1972

Mails, Thomas E. *The People Called Apache*, A Rulledge Book, Prentice Hall Inc., Englewood Cliffs, NJ. 1974

Mason, Otis T. *Aboriginal Skin Dressing, A Study Based on Material in the U. S. National Museum*, Report of the Museum. 1889

Miller, Joan R. *Experimental Replication of Early Woodland Vegetable Fiber Slippers*, Southeastern Archaeology Vol. 7, Number 2. 1988

Miller, Joan R. *Baskets For Your Feet*. December 1995

Miller, James. *Braintan Robes Skins and Pelts: Making Beautiful Leather The Natural Way*, Sunborn Inc., 702 North Sixth Street, St. Clair, MI 48079. 1997

Moore, Robert J. Jr. *Native Americans, A Portrait: The Art and Travels of Charles Bird King, George Catlin, and Karl Bodmer*, Stewart, Tabori and Chang, New York, NY. 1997

National Geographic. *The World of the American Indian*, National Geographic Society, Washington, DC. 1974

Norman, Rex Allen. *The 1837 Sketch Book of the Western Fur Trade*, Scurlock Publishing Co. Inc., Rt 5 Box 347-M, Texarkana, Texas 75501. 1996

Ortiz, Alfonso, Volume Editor. *Handbook of North American Indians Volume 9*. Smithsonian Institution, U.S. Government Printing Office, Washington, DC 20402. 1979

Ortiz, Alfonso, Volume Editor. *Handbook of North American Indians Volume 10*. Smithsonian Institution, U.S. Government Printing Office, Washington, DC 20402. 1983

Parks, Willard Z. *Ethnographic Notes on the Northern Paiute of Western Nevada, 1933-1944 Volume 1*, Compiled and edited by Catherine S. Fowler, University of Utah Anthropological Papers, Number 114, University of Utah Press, Salt Lake City, Utah. 1989

Pascua, Maria Parker. *A Makah Village in 1491 Ozette*, National Geographic Magazine, October 1991, National Geographic Society, Washington, DC. October 1991

Paterek, Josephine. *Encyclopedia of American Indian Costume*, ABC - CLIO Inc., 130 Cremona Drive, PO Box 1911, Santa Barbara, California 93116-1911. 1994

Prebble, Donna. *Yamino Kwiti, Boy Runner of Siba*, The Caxton Printers Ltd., Caldwell, Idaho. 1940

Procter and Gamble, Makers of Ivory Soap, Cincinnati, Ohio 45202. 1-800-846-9480

The Readers Digest Association. *Readers Digest Americas Fascinating Indian Heritage*, The Readers Digest Association Inc., Pleasantville, NY. 1978

Riggs, Jim. *Blue Mountain Buckskin, A Working Manual, Dry-Scrape Brain-Tan*. Second Edition, Wallowa, Oregon. 1990

Ritzenthaler, Robert E. and Pat. *Woodland Indians of the Western Great Lakes*, The Natural History Press, Garden City, New York. 1970

Scharfer, Arlington C. "Buckskin Slim." *The Indian Art of Tanning Buckskin*, Schaefer - Knudtson Publications, Roseburg, Oregon 97470. 1973

Spencer, Robert F. and Jesse D. Jennings. *The Native Americans*, Second Edition, Harper and Row Publishers, New York, Hagerstown, San Francisco, London. 1977

Stacy, Susan M., Editor. *Conversations*, a companion Book to Idaho Public Television, *Proceeding On Through a Beautiful Country, a History of Idaho*, Idaho Public Broadcasting Foundation, Boise, Idaho 83725. 1990

Sterling, Mathew W. *Indians of the Americas*, National Geographic Society, Washington, DC. 1955

Stewart, Jack, Curator. *Unpublished Information*, Museum of the Badlands, Theodore Roosevelt Medora Foundation, PO Box 198, Medora, ND 58645. 1997

Strong, Emory. *Stone Age In The Great Basin*, Binford and Mort Publishing, Portland, Oregon. 1969

Suttles, Wayne, Volume Editor. *Handbook of North American Indians Volume 7*, Smithsonian Institution, U.S. Government Printing Office, Washington, DC 20402. 1990

Tait, James A. and Frany Boas. *The Salishan Tribes of the Western Plateaus*, An excerpt from the 45th B.A.E. Annual Report 1927-1928, Facsimile reproduction, The Shorey Bookstore, 815 Third Ave., Seattle, Washington. 1973

Tandy Leather Company. *Sewing with Leather*, Video, Tandy Leather Company, Fort Worth, Texas 76102. 1986

Tandy Leather Company. *Sewing With Leather*, Booklet, Tandy Leather Company, Fort Worth, Texas 76102. 1978

Taylor, Colin F. *Native American Life, The Family, The Hunt, Pastimes and Ceremonies*, Smithmark Publishers, 16 East 32nd Street, New York, NY 10016. 1996

Taylor, Colin F. *Native American Life*, Smithmark Publishers, New York, NY. 1996

Taylor, Colin F. and William C. Sturtevant. *The Native Americans, The Indigenous People of North America*, Smith Mark Publishers Inc., 112 Madison Ave, New York, NY 10016. 1991-1992

Terrell, John Upton. *Apache Chronicle*, World Publishing, Times Minor, New York. 1972

Terrell, John Upton. *American Indian Almanac*, The World Publishing Company, New York and Cleveland. 1971

Terrell, John Upton. *Sioux Trails*, McGraw-Hill Book Company, New York, St. Louis, San Francisco. 1974

Time-Life Books, The Editors. *The First Americans*, Silver Burdett Company, Morristown, NJ 07960. 1973

Trenholm, Virgina Cole and Maurine Carley. *The Shoshonies: Sentinals of the Rockies*, University of Oklahoma Press, Norman Publications, Division of the University. 1964

Trigger, Bruce G., Volume Editor. *Handbook of North American Indians Volume 15*, Smithsonian Institution, U.S. Government Printing Office, Washington, DC 20402. 1978

Tunis, Edwin. *Indians*, Thomas Y Crowell, 10 East 53 Street, New York, New York. 1959 and 1979

Underhill, Ruth M. *Red Mans America*, The University of Chicago Press, Chicago. 1953

Waldman, Carl. *Atlas of the North American Indian*, Facts On File Publications, New York, NY. 1985

Wallace, Ernest and E. Adamson Hoebel. *The Comanche: Lords of the South Plains*, University of Oklahoma Press, Norman. 1952

Warner, John Anson. *The Life and Arts of the North American Indians*, Crescent Books. 1975

Watson, Don. *Indians of the Mesa Verde*, Cushing - Malloy, Inc., Ann Arbor, Michigan. 1961

Wegner, Gilbert R. *The Story of Mesa Verde National Park*, Mesa Verde Museum Association Inc., Mesa Verde National Park, Colorado 81330. 1980

Wheat, Margaret M. *Survival Arts of the Primitive Paiutes*, University Of Nevada Press, Reno, Nevada. 1967

Whipple, Lieutenant A. W., Thomas Ewbank, Esq. and Prof. William W. Turner. *Reports of Explorations and Surveys to Ascertain the Most Practical and Economical Route For a Railroad from the Mississippi River to the Pacific Ocean Vol. III Part III,* Report Upon The Indian Tribes, Washington Beverly Tucker Printers. 1856

White, George M. *Craft Manual of North American Footwear.* 1969

White, John Manchip. *Everyday Life of the North American Indians*, Holms and Meier Publishers Inc., 30 Irving Place, New York, NY 10003. 1979

Wilbur, C. Keith. *Indian Handicrafts, How to Craft Dozens of Practical Objects Using Traditional Indian Techniques*, The Globe Pequot Press, 6 Business Park Road, Old Saybrook, Connecticut 06475. 1990

Wissler, Clark. *Indians of the Plains*, American Museum of Natural History, Handbook Series No.1, Lancaster Press Inc., Lancaster, PA. 1934

Wissler, Clark. *Indians of the United States*, Doubleday Inc., Garden City, New York. 1966

Womans Day. *101 Gifts to Make*, Page 154, October 25, 1983.

163

Wood, James S. *The Attack on the Belle St. Louis (The Gallant Conduct of Majors Beeler and Smith)*, Letter to the Editor of the Missouri Democrat, October 31, 1864. Letter retyped by Gale Whitmore and in the hands of his son Tony Whitmore of Holister, Idaho.

zu Wied, Prince Maximilian. *People of the First Man, Life among the Plains Indians in their Final Days of Glory*, Promontory Press, New York, NY. 1982

THE TECHNIQUE OF NORTH AMERICAN INDIAN BEADWORK
By
MONTE SMITH

This informative and easy to read book was written by noted author and editor Monte Smith and contains complete instructions on every facet of doing beadwork. Included is information on selecting beads; materials used (and how to use them); designs, with a special emphasis on tribal differences; step-by-step instructions on how to make a loom, doing loom work and the variations of loom work; applique stitches including the lazy stitch, "crow" stitch, running stitch, spot stitch and return stitch; bead wrapping and peyote stitch; how to make rosettes; making beaded necklaces; and, a special section on beadwork edging. There is also a section of notes, a selected bibliography and an index.

The book features examples and photos of beadwork from 1835 to the present time from twenty-three Tribes.

Anyone interested in the craft work of the North American Indian will profit from owning this book.

B00/02 - $13.95

VOICES OF NATIVE AMERICA:
Native American Instruments and Music
By
DOUGLAS SPOTTED EAGLE.

Douglas Spotted Eagle, celebrated flutist and Grammy winning recording artist, performs his Native American music around the world. His book not only provides a much needed discussion of the instruments and musical forms, it also gives the reader a sense of the emotion, complexity and beauty of Native American music from the perspective of a musician. The book is lavishly illustrated and contains many wonderful photographs of Native American musicians and instruments. After providing an overview of Native American music today, Spotted Eagle discusses Flutes, Drums, Rattles, Gourds, Shakers, Whistles, Rasps, Bullroarers, Snapsticks, and Fiddles. Each chapter describes the various types of each instrument and how they are made and used. The flute chapter contains a section on playing techniques. A must for those interested in music or Native American arts & culture.

B00/29 - $17.95

EAGLE'S VIEW PUBLISHING BEST SELLERS

❑ **The Technique of Porcupine Quill Decoration**/Orchard	B00/01	$9.95
❑ **Technique of North American Indian Beadwork**/Smith	B00/02	$13.95
❑ **Techniques of Beading Earrings** by Deon DeLange	B00/03	$9.95
❑ **More Techniques of Beading Earrings** by Deon DeLange	B00/04	$9.95
❑ **Crow Indian Beadwork**/Wildschut and Ewers	B00/06	$10.95
❑ **New Adventures in Beading Earrings** by Laura Reid	B00/07	$9.95
❑ **Beads and Beadwork of the American Indian** by Orchard	B00/08	$16.95
❑ **Traditional Indian Crafts** by Monte Smith	B00/10	$12.95
❑ **Traditional Indian Bead & Leather Crafts**/ Smith/VanSickle	B00/11	$9.95
❑ **Indian Clothing of the Great Lakes: 1740-1840**/Hartman	B00/12	$14.95
❑ **Shinin' Trails: A Possibles Bag of Fur Trade Trivia** by Legg	B00/13	$8.95
❑ **Adventures in Creating Earrings** by Laura Reid	B00/14	$9.95
❑ **Circle of Power** by William Higbie	B00/15	$8.95
❑ **Etienne Provost: Man of the Mountains** by Jack Tykal	B00/16	$9.95
❑ **A Quillwork Companion** by Jean Heinbuch	B00/17	$12.95
❑ **Making Indian Bows & Arrows...The Old Way**/Spotted Eagle	B00/18	$12.95
❑ **Making Arrows...The Old Way** by Doug Wallentine	B00/19	$4.50
❑ **How to Tan Skins the Indian Way** by Evard Gibby	B00/21	$4.95
❑ **A Beadwork Companion** by Jean Hienbuch	B00/22	$12.95
❑ **Beads and Cabochons** by Patricia Lyman	·B00/23	$10.95
❑ **Voices of Native America** by Douglas Spotted Eagle	B00/29	$17.95
❑ **Hemp Masters** by Max Lunger	B00/31	$13.95
❑ **Plains Indian and Mountain Man Crafts I** by C Overstreet	B00/34	$13.95
❑ **Beaded Treasure Purses** by Deon DeLange	B00/42	$10.95
❑ **The Art of Simulating Eagle Feathers** by Gutierrez	B00/43	$9.95
❑ **Eagle's View Publishing Catalog of Books**	B00/99	$4.00

• •

At your local bookstore or use this handy form for ordering:

EAGLE'S VIEW PUBLISHING READERS SERVICE, DEPT TIC
6756 North Fork Road - Liberty, Utah 84310

Please send me the above title(s). I am enclosing $_____
(Please add $3.50 per order to cover shipping and handling.) Send check or money
order - no cash or C.O.D.s please.

Ms./Mrs./Mr. _____

Address _____

City/State/Zip Code _____

Prices and availability subject to change without notice. Please allow three to four
weeks for delivery.

TCNA-6/01